THE 250 RETIREMENT QUESTIONS EVERYONE SHOULD ASK

David Rye, M.B

Avc

Published by Adams Business
An imprint of Adams Media, an F+W Publications Company
57 Littlefield Street, Avon, MA 02322. U.S.A.
www.adamsmedia.com

ISBN 13: 978-1-59869-210-5
ISBN 10: 1-59869-210-0

Printed in the United States.

J I H G F E D C B A

Library of Congress Cataloging-in-Publication Data

Rye, David E.
The 250 retirement questions everyone should ask /
by David Rye & and Kori Bowers.
p. cm.
Includes index.
ISBN-13: 978-1-59869-210-5 (pbk.)
ISBN-10: 1-59869-210-0 (pbk.)
1. Retirement—United States—Planning. 2. Retirement—Economic aspects—United States. 3. Retirement income—United States—Planning. I. Bowers, Kori. II. Title.
HQ1063.2.U6R93 2007
332.02400973—dc22 2007015714

This book is available at quantity discounts for bulk purchases.
For information, call 1-800-289-0963.

CONTENTS

Part IV: Putting It All Together

INTRODUCTION

The numbers are huge—over the next five years, 67 *million* baby boomers will retire. Some are prepared to take the leap, but unfortunately, most of them are still seeking answers to their many questions about retirement before they retire. This book is tailor-made for individuals who have a common goal: to retire. It tells how to master the latest retirement fundamentals and techniques quickly, without wasting time chasing theoretical concepts. It's full of real-world examples and advice, supplemented with a rich menu of easy-to-use Web sites that offer a wealth of additional information.

The book addresses all of the critical retirement questions that are on everyone's mind. Can you afford to retire? How much money will you need? If you die first, will there be enough left over to support your spouse? Should you consider ways to supplement your retirement income? Should you sell your home and buy a cheaper one? How do you protect your estate from federal estate taxes? What kinds of insurance will you need and can you afford it?

Also, retirement is supposed to be an enjoyable time. Enjoyment, however, requires disposable income, and that requires financial planning. Is that vacation home or recreational vehicle that you've always dreamed about practical? Can you afford to travel to your favorite places, and where do you look to find bargain travel deals?

If it is handled right, retirement can be one of the most exciting chapters in your life. However, if your retirement is not planned correctly, it can unravel and you could suddenly discover that you don't have enough money to continue living the lifestyle you've grown accustomed to. The lack of a solid investment plan or sudden unexpected medical expenses, for example, can devastate your savings. This book gives you practical, applicable advice so you can stay ahead of the curve.

PART I

Getting Ready to Retire

Chapter 1

ASSESSING THE BASICS

Retirement has become a norm in our society. Millions of Americans long for the day when they can quit their jobs and turn to a life of fun and leisure. However, many will experience a delay in retirement. Contributing factors such as inadequate retirement savings, stagnating pension benefits, and certain cuts in retirement health benefits are just a few factors prolonging people's retirement plans. Because of this, many potential retirees are choosing to work well into their retirement. In fact, a new Rose Community Foundation study of Denver metro-area residents ranging from 55 to 65 years old found that only 39 percent of the 1,021 people surveyed plan to retire. According to the *Denver Post* newspaper article entitled "Most Boomers Not Ready To Retire" posted on June 27, 2007, the majority are planning to work either part time or full time. The study went on to show that race, ethnicity, and income level all played a key role in these findings. The survey concluded that only 23.3 percent of African-American respondents plan to retire in 10 years as compared to 33 percent for Latinos and 37 percent of Caucasians.

"This generation wants choice. They almost demand choice," said Sheila Bugdanowitz, of the Rose Community Foundation, a philanthropic organization that focuses on programs catering to the aging and education. This chapter will provide questions and answers to help you with the many choices and decisions that need to be made in order to retire at your level of comfort.

Question 1: **Am I ready to take the leap and retire?**

If you answered this question with "I think so" or "No," you've got a problem. You want to *know* that you are ready to retire. Sure, you may not have 100 percent of your retirement bases covered, but you should know what you do and don't have covered. That will give you a chance to put together an action plan that addresses all of your issues. To help you get started, we have created a questionnaire that looks at some of the open questions you may face.

Retirement Qualification Questionnaire

Answer "yes" or "no" to each question. "Maybe" answers are not allowed.

- Do you have any children or other dependents that you must take care of after you retire?
- If yes, do you have a plan in place for how you'll handle this?
- If you retire before you are eligible for Medicare (age 65), will you have medical insurance that covers you?
- Have you explored medical insurance options and cost?
- Do you know the basics about what long-term care insurance covers?
- Do you need life insurance? If you answered yes, then how much?
- Do you know how much money you'll need to support a retirement lifestyle that's acceptable to you?
- Have you identified the exact sources of income that you expect to receive after you retire?

- Do you have a financial contingency plan in place if one or more of your financial sources does not meet your expectations?
- Have you developed a retirement plan that clearly identifies what you want to accomplish before and after you retire?
- Have you created an estate plan that includes the necessary legal documents such as a will?
- Have you reviewed your retirement plan with anybody who is qualified to offer you expert advice?

If our retirement questionnaire created more questions in your mind than answers, then you may want to concentrate your efforts on the questions in the book that address your specific concerns.

Question 2: **My friends keep telling me it's important that I become a millionaire before I retire. Is it?**

That is more of a rhetorical question in line with what your level of comfort is during retirement. The following questions in this book will help you to understand if you truly need to become "a millionaire" before you retire.

Question 3: **What is the greatest fear people have when they retire?**

There's no question that the biggest fear for people when it comes to retirement is financial. Will they have enough money to support themselves and their dependents throughout their retirement years? According to *Forbes* magazine, most people fail to meet their monthly expenses *within the first year* after they retire.

Many retirees fail because they didn't have plans or specific goals before they retired. Be careful not to fall into that same trap. You can head off the biggest fear by saving enough money to retire comfortably.

Question 4: **What do people who successfully retire have in common?**

We can't repeat it enough. To be successful, you have to have a financial plan. We've outlined six steps that people who have successfully retired proactively took to ensure the financial success of their retirement.

Step #1: Diversification Strategy
Before you invest in anything, decide how you want to diversify your portfolio. Your diversification plan should be in place before you make your first investment. You can read more about diversification planning in Chapter 9.

Step #2: Emergency Fund
Create an emergency fund. Unexpected expenses can include uninsured medical costs, auto repairs, and unemployment. Your goal here may be to pay all your monthly bills without relying on future cash sources such as bonuses or credit to cover routine expenses. Make sure you have insurance to cover disability, health, life, automobiles, and your personal property.

Step #3: Credit Cards
Be careful with how you use your credit cards. If you use credit cards to pay for everything and struggle to pay the monthly balance off, then you have a challenge. Consider changing your spending habits so that you can pay off high-interest credit cards each month before you begin investing.

Step #4: Retirement Accounts
If you have retirement accounts such as IRAs, make sure you're making full independent contributions to these accounts before you start investing in anything else. If you have a pension plan in place with your current employer, make sure you know exactly what it will be worth before you retire. For example, if you have determined that you'll need $50,000 of income a year to retire, and you feel

confident that you can, on average, earn 10 percent on your investments, then you'll need $500,000 in your retirement account.

Step #5: Own a Home

If you don't own a home, buy one. It is one of the best tax shelters you can get, and unless you are in a depressed area of the country, you should enjoy appreciation on just about any home you buy, particularly if you are willing to buy in a low market and wait to sell until the market is in an upswing. The other thing to consider when purchasing a home is to buy the lowest priced home in the neighborhood. This can yield the highest appreciation for the owner and all the expenditures in necessary repairs, maintenance, and upkeep will render more profit to you in the end because you have more potential for appreciation.

Step #6: Invest

Learn all you can by reading and studying everything you can get your hands on about investing. Learn about short-term and long-term investment options so that you can decide which investments are best for you. Read more about investments in Chapter 9.

Question 5: **What is a retirement plan, and how do I get one started?**

A retirement plan is the road map that will lead you into retirement. To begin your plan, you need to determine a good tool that you can use. There are literally hundreds of Web sites that have been created to assist individuals in all aspects of retirement planning. Some offer specific retirement advice or special services, while others offer information exchanges between yourself and others. We've listed several of the better sites in our appendix to give you an idea of what's out there and to assist you in your retirement planning efforts.

One particular favorite is Fidelity Investments's Web site because it offers several services that are available to individuals, even if you are not a Fidelity client. To access the site, enter *www.fidelity.com* in your browser. On the top of their home page, select the Retirement and Guidance option. It is a good starting point and provides you access to a complete menu of basic retirement issues that you may want to review.

Question 6: **What are some good sources that I can use to help me prepare for my retirement?**

Many sources are available to help you prepare. We've listed some of our favorites for your convenience. If you enjoy reading books, try Barnes & Noble's Web site (*www.barnesandnoble.com*) or Amazon's Web site (*www.amazon.com*) and browse through their investment book sections. If you prefer researching online and want to find valuable Web sites to search, purchase a copy of *Web Bound* by A. Maccameron. It's a book that lists more than 60,000 Web addresses alphabetically, including a senior citizens' section with numerous sites and a brief description of each site.

Another source is Charles Schwab, which will help you develop a retirement plan with their online calculators, tools, and advice. Go to their home page at *www.schwab.com* and click on Planning and Retirement at the top of the menu. This section should help you get started.

Question 7: **Who can I call on to objectively review my plan before I implement it?**

After you've put your entire retirement plan together in written form, you are ready for a "critical evaluation" of your plan. If you haven't documented your plan in writing, complete with spreadsheets that project income and expenses throughout your retirement, then you don't have a plan that's worth considering. Verbal plans that are hidden in your head are in the same category as pipe dreams.

When you are confident that you have a solid plan, have it ·ed by a professional, such as a CPA, accountant or certified ·l planner. Of course, this review will cost you money up front. However, think about it as a small price to pay to ensure that your plan is solid and tight. You don't want to learn the hard way and find financial holes in your plan once you're into your retirement.

If you are not 150 percent confident that the final written plan will work, then don't do it. It's okay to include contingency plans in your master retirement plan if certain assumptions that you have made don't work out. In fact, if you don't have lots of contingencies built into your plan, you probably don't have a solid plan.

Question 8: **Based on my current age, how should I structure my retirement plan?**

The best way to answer this question is to have you go through the process of creating a plan based on where you are right now and where you hope to be at retirement. However, if you would like to get some preliminary information, you can do a quick fifteen-minute retirement plan review by going to *www.money.cnn.com* and searching for the *Money* magazine article, "The 15-Minute Retirement Plan" or going directly to *http://money.cnn.com/2004/03/10/retirement/investing_15minute_0404/index.htm*. Whether you're starting out or well on your way, the simple rules covered in these retirement plan guidelines will help you get started.

Question 9: **What can I do now to have my finances in order before and after I retire?**

Max out your retirement savings. With most of your major expenses hopefully behind you, it's time to push the savings throttle down and maximize your allowable contributions in your retirement plans (401(k), IRA, etc.). If you are 50-plus, you can start taking advantage of what is called catch-up contributions, which allow you to contribute an extra $5,000 in your 401(k) and an extra $1,000 in a Roth IRA. That's a total of $20,000 through your employee 401(k) contribution of $15,000 and an additional $5,000 for your catch-up contribution. You can also have up to $5,000 for a Roth IRA by adding your $4,000 from your Roth IRA rollover to the $1,000 from your catch-up Roth IRA contribution. If you don't have a Roth IRA or 401(k) account, consider opening one.

As if saving for retirement wasn't hard enough, using the money you've saved will present you with a new set of challenges. As a general rule, tap your tax-deferred accounts last. Generally, it makes sense to withdraw money from your taxable accounts (stocks, mutual funds, etc.) first and let your tax-deferred accounts, such as your IRA, continue to grow as long as possible. You're required to begin withdrawing funds from traditional IRA and 401(k) plans when you turn 70½. Roth IRAs have no mandatory withdrawal requirements.

Question 10: **I've procrastinated about saving money for my retirement. Can you show me how to jump-start my savings plan?**

Start by tracking your daily expenses on a card that you carry with you, or download a free expense worksheet from the AARP's site (*www.aarpmagazine.org/money*). Then, begin by writing down every penny you spend. Look for at least five expenses you can cut that will immediately start saving you money. For example, review your cell phone bill, extracurricular spending, unnecessary luxuries, etc. If you have accumulated some major debt, then your first priority should be to pay off the debt and avoid any additional debt.

If you need an extra incentive to see how much saving a few dollars a day can transform your financial future, use the calculator at *www.aarpmagazine.org/money*. For instance, let's say you came up with ways to save $10 per day or $70 a week. If you invested that $70 savings every week in an investment that, on average, returns 8 percent annually, you would have saved $2,816 in one year. After five years, you would have $16,470. That number would climb to more than $40,000 in ten years.

Question 11: **Should I consider putting some or all of my savings in a CD or a money market fund?**

Certificate of deposits (CDs) are a popular choice for people who want total simplicity, no fees, and guaranteed principle plus interest at all times. They are typically issued on a three-month, six-month, one-year, or longer time basis. Short-term CDs (typically three to six months) pay slightly less interest than longer term CDs. If you purchase a CD, you are required to hold on to it until it expires (e.g., for three months or six months) or pay a small penalty for early withdrawal.

Money market funds (MMFs) are a special breed of savings account set up by financial institutions. They pay interest rates that are tied to the overall market interest rates. When you deposit money into an MMF account, your money begins to immediately earn interest at the current money market rate. And you can withdraw part or all of your deposit in an MMF at any time without incurring an early-withdrawal fee.

In our opinion, the "no penalty" withdrawal feature gives the edge to MMFs and CDs. Both pay higher interest rates than passbook savings accounts. We cannot think of any reason why you would want to keep part or all of your savings in a passbook account over a CD or MMF.

Question 12: **I have $25,000 to invest now. Where should I invest it?**

As you get closer to retirement, start shifting your priorities from wealth-building investments to "making it last" investments. Investments that can produce a steady stream of income will become critical in your retirement years.

Bonds are one way to add income at a low risk. T. Rowe Price (800-638-5660) is one of many sources that offer high-quality tax-free municipal bonds that you can buy. Another alternative is to invest in high-dividend blue-chip stocks. For example, J.P. Morgan

Chase (stock exchange symbol JPM) is an internationally recognized bank that pays 3.2 percent annual dividends on its stock.

Make sure you have the time and inclination to research and track any stock you buy, as well as the fortitude to withstand the ups and downs of the stock market. For those who are not interested in tracking the stock market on a regular basis, check out T. Rowe Price's retirement mutual funds (800-638-5660). Their retirement funds invest in a mix of stocks and bonds that get more conservative as you get older. Fidelity's balanced fund works the same way (800-343-3548).

Question 13: **I need to save more money for my retirement. Can you give me some money-saving tips to make that happen?**

- *Stop charging and do not open up any new credit card accounts.* If you are not sure that you have the willpower to stop charging, then destroy any and all cards immediately.
- *Pay any high-interest debts off first.* Organize your outstanding loans from the highest to the lowest interest rates. If possible, increase the amount of your payments against your high-interest loans first to get them paid off.
- *Consider refinancing your home if it can be done at a lower interest rate than the interest rates on your other debts.* Use the money you save to pay off existing debts.
- *Increase your payments.* If you pay a $20 monthly minimum on a $1,000 credit card that charges 18 percent interest, it'll take you ninety-four months to pay the loan off. If you increased the payments to $40 a month, you'll pay the loan off in just thirty-four months and can use the extra money for savings.

- *Consider doing work on the side and put the money you earn into savings.* This will expedite your efforts in reaching your financial retirement goals.

Question 14: **If I decide that I need $5,000 a month to cover my retirement expenses and the standard of living that I've grown accustomed to, how much will I need in my savings account?**

To determine how much you will need in your savings and investment accounts to provide you with an income of $5,000 a month, go to *Money* magazine's Web site at *www.money.cnn.com/retirement/index.html* and use the formula on the right-hand side of the Retirement home page. This will help you determine the amount you'll need to save each month in order to reach your goal.

Chapter 2

BECOMING FINANCIALLY INDEPENDENT

Being financially independent means having the wherewithal to do whatever you want to do, regardless of the cost. Some would argue that only a few people in the world ever achieve the enviable position of truly being financially independent. Perhaps Bill Gates is one of them.

We would argue that being financially independent is more dependent upon one's state of mind than it is on some arbitrary dollar figure. For example, you may have concluded that you would be happy and satisfied with a well-thought-out retirement plan that costs you X dollars to maintain and allows you the added luxuries you desire. Once you have accumulated the necessary dollars to maintain that plan, then you have achieved financial independence.

Question 15: **What does it mean to become financially independent?**

Financial independence means having the wherewithal to say to yourself, "If I wanted to, I could quit my job today and live comfortably off my investments for the rest of my life." If you do the right things, this goal is very obtainable.

However, according to the Social Security Administration, most Americans retire on less than $20,000 a year. These are people just like you, who worked hard all of their lives. The facts are that although most people know how to make money, they either lack the discipline or don't know how to save and invest their money.

Question 16: **What are the basic steps one must take to become financially independent?**

To become financially independent, you must consistently save and invest your money. You need a savings plan that's flexible, but firm, and most important, something you can stick to. Your first challenge will be to get control over your spending habits and establish a monthly budget for everything you buy. If you can start saving on even the little things, it will add up to big dollars over a relatively short period of time. Here are some steps for you to take:

- *Make up a "savings bill."* When it comes time to pay the bills, make sure it's the first bill that gets paid, in the form of a deposit to your savings account. That way, adding money to your savings becomes a top priority.
- *After you pay off all your bills and discover that you have some money left over, make another deposit to your savings account.*
- *Find out if your employer's payroll system allows you to make direct deposits into a savings account.* If it does, sign up for the program today; in a short period of time, you won't even miss the money that's deducted from your paycheck.

- *When you get unexpected money (e.g., a gift, a bonus, tax refunds), deposit it into your savings account so you won't use it to buy something you don't need.*
- *Pay off your home mortgage faster by sending your payment coupons in early along with an extra payment.* This is a wise financial move because you will be charged less interest due to the shortening of your overall home loan.
- *Don't rush out to trade your car in just because the loan is paid off.* There is nothing better than a car that's paid for. If "old faithful" is still running, keep it and save the money.

Question 17: **What steps do I need to take to find out where I am financially today?**

To find out where you are financially, go through your checkbook and write down what you spent your money on over the past three months (e.g., food, entertainment, credit card interest). Often, credit card companies will categorize your purchases for you so that you can see your spending patterns. How much money did you make, and did you have enough to cover all of your expenses? What's your bottom line? Did you spend more than you made? Where did the money go? If you spent less than you made, what did you do with the extra money? Consider these steps:

- *Set financial goals.* To be meaningful, a goal must be very specific, with a designated completion date assigned to it.
- *Cut back on expenses.* If you are living above your means, figure out a way to live below your means. You must figure out how to live on what you make or you will never gain control of your finances.
- *Create a contingency fund.* Your fund should sufficiently cover three to six months of your expenses in case you become unemployed, your car breaks down, or something unexpected comes up.

Question 18: **What resources can I turn to that will show me how to become financially independent?**

Some excellent resources are offered at a minimal cost or free to anyone who is interested. A great Web site that offers a variety of articles pertaining to financial freedom is *www.money.cnn.com*. It may also be worthwhile to consider a subscription to a monthly magazine such as *Fortune* or *Money*. It can be a helpful reminder to keep you on your financial track when you receive the magazine every month through your mail. Of course books on this topic are plentiful and can be checked out at your local library for free or ordered used and at a discounted price through *www.amazon.com*. A couple of suggested books are *The 9 Steps to Financial Freedom* by Suze Orman or *The Six-Day Financial Makeover* by Robert Pagliarini.

Question 19: **You hear a lot about using compound interest to accumulate retirement funds. What is it?**

Compound interest is the interest paid and accumulated on dollars that are invested at a fixed rate of return. So when interest is added to the account balance, the interest earned on the investment earns additional interest during the duration of the investment. This compounding rate is what we classify as compound interest. You may have heard that using compound interest is beneficial for retirement because there are some advantages for savers who choose to use compound interest in their favor. To read and understand this in greater detail, visit *www.banking.about.com* and do a search on compound interest.

Question 20: **How can I use compound interest to achieve financial independence?**

As a saver, you can feel more comfortable using compound interest. Begin to understand how compound interest works and how to use it to get ahead financially. The compound interest "rule of 72" dramatically illustrates how compound interest works. Divide 72 by the yield you expect to make on a given investment. The result is how long it will take to double your money. For example, if you estimate that an investment you own will yield 18 percent annually, then you will double your money in four years (72/18 = 4).

Question 21: **Do I need a budget, and what are the main components of a budget?**

Everyone should have a budget, even millionaires. It is critical to understand where your money is coming from and where is it going. By monitoring your spending habits, you will begin to identify areas where cost savings can occur. Ultimately you will then be able to create a budget that is conducive to your retirement. It will become a tool that you can reference to keep your spending on track that contains your buying, spending, and saving habits.

Question 22: **I know that budgeting takes discipline and commitment. How can I make the process less demanding on my time?**

Find a good resource or tool that is available for you to implement right away. For example, if you go to SimplePlanning.com at *www.simpleplanning.net*, they have a program that is downloadable for a flat fee that is less than $10. If you are using Microsoft Office, then consider using the financial templates that are included in the program. Any financial planning tool will help organize your spending and make the process less demanding on your personal time.

Question 23: **What money-saving steps can I take to help me reach my retirement goal?**

After you complete your budget, you will probably start to see some money-saving areas within your personal realm that you can tackle right away. Above and beyond the saving you may uncover in your budget, begin thinking about these three simple steps:

- *Identify what are necessary expenses and what are luxury expenses.* For example, does each family member really need a cell phone? Do you truly need the glorified cable television package?
- *Closely review your miscellaneous spending.* Is there anything that you can do away with? Do you see any patterns in your spending behavior that you can begin to address?
- *Prioritize your budget.* Consider categorizing the most important to least important expenditures you have. Then begin assessing what you can do away with or cut back on.

Chapter 3

AVOIDING DEBT TRAPS

Achieving financial independence when you're up to your neck in debt may make the goal seem impossible to reach. Vow to become debt-free in a year and list the steps you'll take to make that happen. To learn more about becoming debt-free, pick up a copy of *Life Without Debt* by Bob Hammond.

Question 24: **I'm spending every dime I make. What can I do to get my expenses under control before I retire?**

This is where your budget will really come in handy. Understanding your expenses and where they are coming from will be your first step in getting them under control. The budget will help you to outline your expenses and identify any areas that can be eliminated. For example, do you really need to have Starbucks coffee every day? At $3 a day, that's $1,095 a year! Budgeting will also flag some necessary expenses and you can begin to think about how you can decrease them.

Question 25: **Do I need to know what my expenses are today and project what they will be when I retire?**

This is a great question to ask yourself, and your budget will help with comparing what your expenses are today versus what they are projected to be in retirement. For example, one expense you have today might be your high Internet bill that is necessary for your current job role. However, after retirement, you may not need high speed Internet and may be able to consider doing away with or lessening this expense because the need will go away. The same goes for things such as multiple phone lines and cell phones required for your current job. You may not need all of these services when you retire. Identifying these items now will help you forecast for your actual retirement expenditures.

Question 26: **Are there any outside sources that I can use to help me quantify my post-retirement expenses?**

Be very realistic as to what your retirement expenses are expected to be. A good expense budget calculator is on the Internet at the following location: *http://cgi.money.cnn.com/tools/instantbudget/instantbudget_101.jsp*.

Question 27: **Why do people buy a lot of stuff that they really don't need in retirement?**

Competing with the Jones's is one reason. There is always a "latest and greatest" for any product, and if this is your thing, then you'll pay for it. Let's look at televisions. In less than two years, plasma television prices have been cut in half. Another good example is the latest, hottest, fastest computer technology, which costs plenty at first but then plummets in price in a matter of months. What's key to avoiding debt is to hold off on any frivolous spending. Apply any extra money you may have toward paying off your debt before you decide to accumulate more debt. According to *Money* magazine's October 2005 issue, the average credit card debt per American household was $9,312. Avoid this trap by simply adhering to your budget.

Question 28: **How can I avoid credit and loan traps that may stifle my retirement?**

Inappropriate use of credit and loans can become one of your biggest financial downfalls. When your wallet is nearly empty and your checkbook balance is low, you know you're nearing your spending limit. But if you can easily turn to credit, you are more likely to overspend without realizing it—until the bills start coming in. Most financial counselors recommend that you stop charging when your credit payments (not including a mortgage) approach 15 to 20 percent of your take-home pay. To determine whether you owe too much, check the following warning signs:

1. You're always juggling payments or stalling one creditor to pay another.
2. You're consistently receiving past due notices on your bills.
3. You fail to save a set amount of money each month.
4. You're charging more each month than you make in monthly payments.
5. You're taking longer and longer to pay off your debts.

Question 29: **I'm spending a fortune on credit cards. What steps can I take now, before I retire, to get off the cards?**

Wonderful things will happen to you once you kick the credit card habit. You'll start buying less of what you really don't need. Each card has a limit to the amount of credit you can get. If you have many credit accounts, the total limit available to you may be more than you can handle. So it's really up to you to establish the credit limit that you can realistically handle. The first step is to determine what your personal credit limit should be by figuring out how much you can afford to pay each month for credit purchases. Once you establish your personal credit limit, plan your credit spending so that your total payments cover, at a minimum, your credit purchases plus interest.

The second step is to limit yourself to one or two cards. You should consider the cards that are widely accepted throughout the world, and get the ones with the best interest rates. Next, record everything you charge in a memo book so you know where you are at any time during the month. You may be able to do this step online by viewing your account activities on your card's Web site. This will eliminate surprises at the end of the month when you get your bill and exclaim, "Wow, I didn't realize I spent that much."

If you are truly in debt with your cards, and struggle not to use them, then you may have to get rid of your cards altogether. Depending on your situation, you may want to look into getting a consolidation loan to pay them off.

Question 30: **What are the different kinds of credit cards? Which one should I use?**

Several different kinds of credit cards are made available to the general public. Some have lower interest rates, but you pay an annual fee. Other varieties offer competitive interest rates, but vary in their features. The best way to find out all the options and choose the best one for you is at *www.e-wisdom.com*. This site offers personalized recommendations, based on information you supply, and shows comparison charts so that you can see the differences between all the cards offered. You may also choose to look at *www.cardratings.com*, which offers a variety of resources to help you understand everything related to credit cards.

Question 31: **If I want to borrow money, what are the best ways to do it?**

The best way to borrow money is through whatever means is available to you that offers the lowest interest rate possible. If you can borrow from a friend or family member who will charge you no interest, then take it. If you have to go with a source that will require you to pay interest, then do your research to find the best rate available. Depending on the amount of money you need (which may be better answered in our next question) you can look at the low-interest incentives offered through your current credit card or home equity line of credit, or consider borrowing from a friend who will charge you minimal interest.

Question 32: **If I decide to purchase a big-ticket item in retirement, what is the best way to pay for it?**

There are several good ways to pay for big-ticket items. Cash is preferred. If you can't pay for something with cash, you should reconsider whether you really need this item. If you use your credit card, it should only be because you are in a situation where you can't use cash, and you know that you will be able to pay off the bill in full at the end of the month, before interest starts accruing.

Another option is to borrow money. However, borrowed money typically comes with a price. Generally this is in the form of an interest rate, so you want to be careful of the rate offered and how it works. For example, if you decide to buy a new car, there may be several car companies that offer low interest rates to buyers. Just make sure you read the fine print in any deal that you sign up for.

Question 33: **I'm thinking about replacing my car once I retire. Should I buy a new one?**

According to the U.S. Department of Transportation, the total cost of driving a car 25,000 miles annually is $7,500, or about 30 cents a mile. Car payments are not included in their calculation, but depreciation is a big part of the number. For example, if you purchase a new car for $25,000, it's estimated that your car instantly depreciates by about $5,000 as soon as you drive it off the car lot.

Before you set out to buy a car, decide what kind of vehicle you need and what options are necessary. Consider fuel efficiency, seating capacity, overall size, your use of this car, and so on. Once you have your list, begin your research. For a comprehensive car-buying guide, go to *www.intellichoice.com/info/about_intellichoice*. Another great online resource is *www.edmunds.com*.

Question 34: **What factors should I consider if I decide to lease a car?**

Some people think that leasing is not substantially different than financing a car, and because monthly lease payments are typically lower than what it costs to finance a car, they assume that leasing is the less expensive option. However, that may not be the case. Leasing a vehicle is very different from buying one. When you lease, you are, in effect, renting a car for a specified period of time. Because you don't own it, you are obligated, under a lease contract, to maintain the vehicle and drive it a limited number of miles per year. If you try to get out of a lease before it expires, you will be required to pay significant penalty costs.

Take a moment to answer the following questions to determine whether leasing is a viable option for you:

- Do you typically trade in a new car every four years or less?
- Do you, on average, drive fewer than 15,000 miles a year?
- Do you need a new car every few years for whatever reason?

If you answered "yes" to one or more of these questions, then you might want to consider leasing. Shop around and get lease contract details and bids from at least two dealers on the vehicle you want.

Question 35: **What are the advantages and disadvantages of buying a used car?**

Over a five-year period, a new car will depreciate an estimated 30 to 50 percent. Most of the depreciation occurs within the first two years. Therefore, an advantage is to consider buying a used vehicle that's three or four years old. That way, you are not experiencing the depreciation and actually benefit from someone else's loss. A good way to determine how much the car you are considering depreciates is to go to *www.edmunds.com*. Review what the new cost of the model would be versus what value it holds after two, three, or four years. This may help you decide whether you would like to buy this car new or used.

Chapter 4

FINDING THE BEST PLACES TO LIVE

There are some wonderful places to retire in America, and the list gets broader and broader every year. The best way to begin your quest is to identify some areas of interest. A variety of hot spots have popped up all over the United States that are geared toward the retirement population. In fact, *Money* magazine publishes an annual edition that covers the best places to retire in America. The magazine polled its readers to determine where the baby boomers want to retire. The number-one choice for the readers was to stay in their current location. The runner-up was to move closer to their children. The third choice was to have a second home. Whatever scenario fits your bill, knowing your options is key in your decision-making process.

Question 36: **Where are the best places to retire in the United States?**

To help you determine what areas interest you, take a few minutes to complete the quiz found at *www.findyourspot.com*. The quiz takes you through a series of questions to help narrow your results to areas that might appeal to you. Don't forget, you now have the time to check out each area if you want. You can even spend some time at each destination and really determine whether the community is right for you.

Question 37: **If I decide to relocate, what geographic attributes should I consider?**

A helpful resource that will give you several factors to consider geographically is at *http://money.cnn.com/best/bpretire*. This Web site offers several tools to get you started on your quest. You can enter cities and find out all the statistics related to your search. For example, a search on San Diego, California, yields the population of the city, median price for a house, average income of the area, etc. You can also check out the retirement planning sections of the site and determine how much you could sell your house for, learn how to find your dream home and location, get financial strategies, and much more.

Question 38: **If I decide to move, should I rent or buy a home?**

According to the late Andrew Carnegie, "ninety percent of all millionaires became so through owning real estate." He went on to state that "more money has been made in real estate than in all industrial investments combined." What Carnegie, as well as other investors, would tell you is to buy a home if you don't already have one. Wells Fargo has an extensive site about home buying, including workshops and seminars for the prospective home buyer. To help you get started, go to *www.wellsfargo.com/challenge*. A great book to pick up is *Buy Your First Home* by Robert Irwin.

On the contrary, if you decide to rent, understand that you are paying someone else's mortgage and helping her to experience the appreciation and tax advantages on the property. However, renting is sometimes advantageous when you move to a new area and are not sure where you want to live, or if you decide to build a house and need temporary shelter during the process. We don't rule out renting because it really depends on your situation and needs. We just suggest that you weigh the pros and cons of owning versus renting to determine what solution works best for you in retirement.

Question 39: **If I decide to move, should I consider buying a condominium or a house?**

Condominiums are attached to one another, thereby sharing common walls. You own a unit and share common grounds such as recreational areas with the other condominium owners through what is called a homeowners' association. One of the major advantages condominiums have over freestanding homes is that they generally cost less to buy and require less upkeep. Each owner pays a monthly maintenance fee to the homeowners' association to maintain the exterior walls of each condominium, provide landscaping services, and pay for some form of homeowner's insurance.

Condominium covenants typically have a long list of things you can and can't do as an owner. If you don't like regulations, don't buy a condominium. For retired people, condos offer a comfortable step back from what it takes to care for a home. Security is generally tighter in a condominium complex than it is around a private home because of the close proximity of neighbors. Some condominiums have twenty-four-hour security guards on the premises.

Single-family homes generally have a greater potential for capital appreciation than condominiums if they're located in an area where property values have consistently risen over the past several years. Quite often, small investments in cosmetic improvements such as paint and landscaping can substantially improve their selling price. They offer more privacy than what you will find in a condominium since you are not in such close proximity to your neighbors. And if gardening and landscaping is your forte, then a home with a backyard might be better for you. However, since you are responsible for all upkeep on a home, you can expect to spend more to maintain a home than you would a condominium. The decision ultimately comes down to personal preference. You really can't go wrong with either one. You have to weigh it all out and determine what's right for you.

Question 40: **I have a lot of equity in my home. Should I keep my house or sell it?**

Although you probably bought your home years ago, thanks to inflation you've ended up with an asset that's worth a lot more than what you paid for it. Over the past three decades, the rise in single-family home prices has become the cornerstone of many Americans' retirement nest egg. The opportunity to leverage the equity they've built up in their homes has become the foundation of their retirement plans. As you approach retirement, consider these options when you evaluate whether you should keep or sell your home:

- *Consider trading down.* Estimate your profit before you consider selling. What will it cost for an acceptable replacement? If the potential profit from selling your home is minimal, it might not be worth the effort of trading down.
- *Time the sale of your home to take advantage of tax breaks.* If you or your spouse is age 55 or older, you can exclude from taxes up to $500,000 of the capital gains on the sale of your home.
- *Consider keeping your home and refinancing it with an individual reverse mortgage (IRM) or a leaseback.* In this arrangement, a lender receives part or all of the equity in your home, in return for payments that you receive for the rest of your life.
- *Sell your home and move to a part of the country where the costs of housing and living are lower.* Not only will you get more home for your money, you may also get the added benefit of a lower cost of living in the new area.

Question 41: **Should I consider living in a retirement community?**

Throughout the country, retirement communities have popped up that offer all levels of care for the aging population. With a boomer turning age 50 every eight seconds, the demand for these retirement developments has skyrocketed. One site that can help you search the market is *www.seniorhousingnet.com*. The site offers a one-stop shop for resources on retirement. It provides information and tips about housing, moving, financing, and specialized care and is a wealth of knowledge at your fingertips.

Question 42: **If I decide to remodel and improve my home, what can I do to get the most out of the money I spend?**

The house you have always dreamed of may be the one you already live in. Maybe you're thinking of a spacious living room, a modern kitchen, or an extra bath. If so, turning your vision into reality may simply be a matter of remodeling your present house. But, whatever you do, you want to make sure you can get your money back out of your investment should you decide to sell your home. Consider the following things before you decide to remodel:

- *Highest returns.* Popular improvements such as remodeling a bath or a kitchen add the most value and will usually yield great returns when you sell your home.
- *Energy efficiency.* Installing energy-improvement devices is always a good way to reduce your monthly energy costs. Don't install expensive energy-efficient devices unless you plan to stay in you home for at least another three years however.
- *Don't over-improve.* Consider the value of your home in your neighborhood. If you'd have to price your home significantly above the average price range in your neighborhood

to recover your home improvement costs, you may have difficulty selling it later on.

- *General maintenance.* Home maintenance projects, such as roof repair and replacement, are essential whether or not you're anticipating selling your home.

The Home Remodeling Organizer by Robert Irwin discusses various remodeling projects from a practical perspective. Also check out *Squeeze Your Home for Cash: 101 Great Money-Making Ideas for Homeowners* by Ruth Rejnis.

Question 43: **What is the best way to find a good deal on a home?**

Consider buying a "fixer-upper" if you are handy with tools and paintbrushes. A structurally sound house that is priced 20 to 30 percent below market because it needs some "tender loving care" could be a good investment. Look for distress situations where a seller has to put a house on the market for a quick sale because of a job transfer, divorce settlement, or foreclosure to settle an estate. Here are some tips for finding a good deal on a home:

- *If you can, buy the cheapest house in the neighborhood.* The higher-priced homes will tend to pull the value of yours up as they appreciate.
- *Consider what a house looks like on the outside.* Make sure the house you buy has curb appeal or the potential for curb appeal with minor enhancements.
- *Ask the seller to include a home warranty in the selling price when you submit an offer.* A typical warranty covers major home systems such as plumbing, heating, and electrical equipment.
- *Assume a mortgage.* If you can find a seller who wants to get out from under his mortgage due to personal situations, then his mortgage company may be anxious to work with you to prevent a possible foreclosure.

Chapter 5

FINANCING A HOME

Anybody who's thinking about a home mortgage should be prepared to shop aggressively. Some lenders have drastically lower rates and fees than others, especially for preferred borrowers. One percentage point saved on a fifteen-year, $200,000 loan is worth $36,720, or about $210 a month.

Mortgage banks are usually the cheapest route to go. Their main business is mortgages, including those that are backed by the Federal Housing Administration or the Department of Veterans Affairs. Credit unions are your next-best bet, although only the larger ones offer mortgages. Next, try savings and loan banks and associations followed by commercial banks. As in any field, some mortgage brokers are more competent and attentive than others. And don't be afraid to shop the Web. Many national and regional mortgage banks advertise their rates and services complete with applications online.

Question 44: I want to pay off my mortgage as quickly as possible. Will I save anything?

Nothing can save you more money than paying off your home mortgage as soon as you can. Typically, people opt for thirty-year mortgages because they give them plenty of time to pay off their homes, while offering them lower monthly payments. However, if you can work it into your budget to have a higher monthly mortgage in order to pay off your home faster, then do so.

If you're buying a house or own a home with a thirty-year mortgage with no prepayment penalties (most don't have them), consider what a fifteen-year mortgage can do for you. For example, if you have a $200,000 thirty-year 7 percent mortgage, your payments are approximately $1,400 a month. If you finance the same amount for fifteen years, your payments would be $1,700 a month. For a difference of only $300 a month, you can pay for your house outright in half the time. If you have a good interest rate with your current thirty-year loan, then consider paying an extra payment each year and you will expedite paying off your home, which can catapult your early retirement ambitions.

Question 45: What are the advantages to paying off my home mortgage early?

Here are three key advantages to paying off your mortgage early:

1. It forces you to save for something you care about, your home, and will substantially reduce the amount of interest you'll pay over time.
2. If you are looking to trade up to a more expensive home, nothing will get you there faster than building equity in your existing house.
3. It offers you an opportunity to be mortgage-free when you retire.

If you want to read more about the advantages of paying off your home earlier than expected, as well as understanding all the types of loans available, then consider reading *The Banker's Secret* by Marc Eisenson.

Question 46: **I have a thirty-year loan. Is there a way that I can accelerate paying off my home with my current loan?**

The best way to pay down your current loan is to make extra payments on your existing loan. If you decide to do this, make sure your lender understands that the extra money you're paying should be applied against the principle and not applied toward a non-interest-bearing impound account, which lenders would prefer. If you can't afford to make the extra monthly payments, make just one extra payment per year, and you'll drop years off your thirty-year mortgage.

Question 47: **When does it pay to refinance a mortgage?**

Mortgage loan experts will tell you to consider refinancing your mortgage when interest rates drop 2 percentage points below your current rate. Before you pursue a refinance option, you need to get answers to several questions from prospective lenders:

- Given the current rates, how much will you save each month after you refinance?
- How much will it cost to refinance and will you be in your home long enough to make it worthwhile?
- Is the term of the proposed refinance plan the same as or less than your current mortgage term?

If you want to compare the effect of different interest rates and terms, run your current mortgage figures through a mortgage calculator found at *www.mortgage-calc.com*. Then run the new figures you're considering to see if they make sense.

Question 48: **I'm not very loan savvy. Can you help me understand the lingo?**

You need to understand several terms when going through the loan or refinance process. We have listed a few to help get you started:

- **Terms:** A term is the amount of time that is set for the repayment of the mortgage or loan. Typically a term ranges from fifteen to thirty years. Review the rate and term of any new loan you're considering. One lender may offer you a lower interest rate but a longer term. Another may offer you a higher rate but shorter term. Shop around and make sure you are comparing apples with apples to find the best deal.
- **Closing costs:** Some mortgage companies offer loans with no closing costs, which are costs owed during the closing of the property. Generally speaking, you'll pay higher interest, but if you're not sure how long you'll be in your home, this may be a good deal. Check the fine print to make sure there are no early prepayment penalties in case you decide to sell.
- **Loan options:** Some mortgage companies offer streamlined loans that allow you to get better rates and/or terms without having to go through all the expensive steps of closing associated with a new appraisal. You'll end up paying lower closing costs but potentially a higher interest rate.
- **Modified loans:** Your existing mortgage company may offer you a modified loan. They may be willing to change your loan rate and/or term by simply modifying your existing loan. Subsequently, a new loan does not need to be created and there is no closing, which eliminates closing costs.

Question 49: **What are some options that I may want to consider if I refinance my home?**

One thing you can look into is writing off points on your tax return when you refinance. Usually the points paid to a mortgage company must be written off over the life of the new loan. But if you refinance a second time before all of the points are written off on your original loan, you can deduct the entire remaining balance in the year that you refinanced. The write-off could amount to several thousands of dollars. To learn more, reference Julie Garton-Good's book *All About Mortgages: Insider Tips to Finance a Home*, which covers everything you need to know about home mortgages. Another excellent reference is *Your Home Mortgage Answer Book: 100 Questions and the Answers You Need* by Mary Callegari, which covers refinancing and mortgage insurance questions. And finally, *The Mortgage Kit* by Thomas Steinmetz and Phillip Whitt gives you a comprehensive guide to everything you ever wanted to know about mortgages.

Question 50: **If I decide to get a home loan, what do I need to do first?**

The first thing is to understand the loans that will be offered to you. Most homes are financed with loans secured by a deed of trust, commonly referred to as a mortgage. Mortgages are available from many sources, including commercial banks, savings and loan associations, credit unions, insurance companies, and mortgage companies. Most lenders offer fully amortized loans in which you repay the principle (borrowed amount) and the interest over a specified period of time. At first, most of your payment goes toward the interest. As you continue to make payments over time, an increasing part of your payment goes to pay off the principle and a decreasing part goes to the interest. Interest is either fixed or variable. Fixed-rate loans are where the interest rate and your monthly payments remain the same over the term of the loan, which is usually thirty years. Variable-rate loans offer an interest rate that fluctuates with the market interest rate. They are usually indexed to the prime rate plus points. The prime rate is the preferred interest rate that is offered by lending institutions to their best corporate customers. The prime rate will fluctuate up or down at any point in time with changes in the economy.

A point is equivalent to one interest point, so if a bank offers you a variable-rate mortgage at prime plus two points, and prime is at 6 percent, you'll pay 8 percent interest. If the prime increases to 7 percent next month, you'll pay 9 percent interest. Because of the variable fluctuations, you need to proceed with caution when choosing this type of loan.

If you want to see what resources are available online, E-Loan at *www.eloan.com* offers mortgages from sixty lenders to home buyers in thirty-nine states. Home Shark at *www.homeshark.com* provides a service that is similar to E-Loan. They represent sixteen lenders who operate out of forty-six states. Quicken Loans at *www.quickenloans.com* offers a service that lets you compare rates and terms with eleven national lenders.

Chapter 6

CHECKING YOUR RETIREMENT ACCOUNT OPTIONS

To be financially prepared for your retirement, it is important that you know about the various types of retirement accounts that may be available to you and what each one has to offer. There are a variety of options and features in the different accounts; you can find the combination that is exactly what you're looking for.

Question 51: **Can you help me understand the different retirement plans that may be available through my employer?**

Employer retirement plans and the tax laws that back them are very complex, so seek outside expertise if you need help determining the best plan for you. Most retirement plans fall into one of two categories: defined benefit or defined contribution.

In a defined benefit plan, the employer commits to the benefit and takes on the responsibility of managing the plan. The benefit is based on what's in the plan when you retire. For example, an employer may define a plan that requires the company to deposit a fixed annual sum of money into the plan for each eligible employee (i.e., a defined benefit). When an employee retires, she is then entitled to the money that the employer deposited on her behalf.

Defined contribution plans outline what the employer's contribution will be, not the benefit to the employee. The plans are usually profit-sharing and/or salary reduction plans. Profit-sharing plans pay into the plan based on a percentage of profits. Obviously, there are no guarantees. If there are no profits, nothing gets paid into the plan.

Defined contribution plans allow employees to set aside income on a pretax basis, such as into a 401(k) plan. Employers can commit to match all or part of an employee's contribution into the plan. Defined contribution plans shift all retirement risks onto the employee. What they accumulate in the plan depends on how much was contributed and how the funds were invested. The retirement plan table below outlines the different options to help you determine the best plan for you.

Quick Rundown on Retirement Plans

Plan Name	Who Qualifies	Best For	Maximum Contribution
401(k)	Employees working for profit businesses	Everyone who qualifies	Up to 15% of salary or $9,500, whichever is less
403(b)	Employees of nonprofit organizations	Everyone who qualifies	Up to 20% of salary or $9,500, whichever is less
IRA	Anyone with earned income	Those who don't have a pension plan or who have put the maximum into their company plans	Up to $5,000 depending on your age

Plan Name	Who Qualifies	Best For	Maximum Contribution
SEP	Self-employed employees	Self-employed person who is a sole proprietor	Up to 13% of self-employment income or $22,500, whichever is less
Profit-sharing Keogh	The self-employed and employees of unincorporated small businesses	Small-business owner who is funding a plan for himself and his employees	Up to 13% of self-employment income or $22,500, whichever is less
Money-purchase Keogh	The self-employed and employees of unincorporated small businesses	Small-business owner who wants to shelter more than what's allowed by profit-sharing Keogh	20% of net self-employment income or $30,000, whichever is less
Defined-purchase Keogh	Same as profit-sharing Keogh	Self-employed person nearing retirement who needs to set aside a high percentage of income	Maximum benefit needed to fund is $120,000 or 3 years' average income, whichever is less
Variable annuity	Anyone	Someone who has put the maximum into other retirement plans and won't need the money for 10 years	No limits
Fixed annuity	Anyone	Someone who has put the maximum into other plans and doesn't like risks	No limits

Question 52: **Are my company's pension plan and private retirement accounts secure? How can I find out?**

To determine whether your plan is safe, consider working with a financial professional and have him go over your plan with you. For a fee, he will make sure that your plan is diverse and that your investments are fairly safe depending on your age, your retirement goals, and the financial stability of the company you work for. For example, if you are getting close to retirement, a financial expert would most likely look for low-risk investments in your retirement accounts. If you are younger and are comfortable with taking risks, he might suggest adding more aggressive investments to your accounts. Having an analysis done on your pension fund will give you peace of mind so that you can sleep at night and be assured that your retirement planning is still on track.

Question 53: **What's a rollover?**

A rollover is a procedure that the IRS designed that allows you to distribute or "roll over" assets from one retirement plan into another. For example, if you change jobs or retire, you can transfer assets from one retirement plan to another—such as from an employer-sponsored 401(k) plan into an IRA—protecting your tax-free status and avoiding any early-withdrawal penalties.

There are several advantages to rolling over your managed IRA plans into a self-directed plan. Self-directed IRAs offer you a range of investment choices such as mutual funds, stocks, bonds, and CDs that are not traditionally offered by managed plans.

Question 54: **What are Simplified Employee Pension plans?**

A Simplified Employee Pension plan, commonly known as a SEP plan, is a retirement plan specifically designed for small-business owners and self-employed individuals. The plan is based on an IRA, and employers can make tax-deductible contributions on behalf of their employees. The eligible individual will not pay taxes on the contribution, but rather on the distribution he receives from the SEP account.

An employer with one or more employees is eligible to open an SEP plan. Even a self-employed individual who is the only employee can qualify for this sort of account. However, an individual employee cannot open her own account. If you need more information regarding SEP plans, feel free to browse *www.investopedia.com.*

Question 55: **What are the key features of SEP plans?**

Key features include:

- Tax-deductible contributions are allowed up to 25 percent of the first $41,000 of your income.
- All investment earnings can grow tax-deferred until withdrawn.
- Employers must contribute the same percentage of contribution to every employee who participates in the SEP plan.
- You can choose from a wide variety of investments for your SEP plan, including mutual funds, stocks, bonds, and CDs.
- There are no complicated forms to fill out when you open a SEP and no annual reports that need to be filed with the IRS.

Question 56: **What are self-employed 401(k) plans?**

Self-employed 401(k) plans were designed for self-employed people who have no employees, other than their spouses, working for them. A summary of the plan's features follows:

- You are allowed to make up to $13,000 in tax-deductible deductions into the plan. If you are older than 50, you can make up to $16,000 in tax-deductible deductions into the plan.
- They offer the highest contribution potential for self-employed individuals.
- Form 5500 must be filed with the IRS annually.

Question 57: **Why are so many people excited about 401(k) plans?**

The 401(k) is probably one of the most powerful tools you have to save for retirement. They're offered through employers and can be contributory or noncontributory. In addition to enabling you to save for retirement, they offer one of the best tax shelters that our federal government has ever managed to create.

Question 58: **What are some steps I can take to improve my 401(k) investment?**

- *Maximize your contribution.* Most companies match some portion of their employees' contributions. If you can't afford to save the maximum, at least contribute enough to take full advantage of your employer's contribution.
- *Make sure you know every investment option in your plan and review how each option is doing at least once a quarter.* Don't be afraid to switch to different options if they are consistently doing better than the original ones you picked.
- *Don't be greedy.* Your 401(k) doesn't have to beat the stock market every year. What's more important is that you get the return you need to build a solid retirement fund.
- *Diversify your plan so that it is not 100 percent susceptible to a specific economic event.* You want to have a healthy mix of stocks and bonds that are balanced.

Question 59: **How does a 401(k) plan work, and how much can I contribute to one?**

Typically, your employer will have all the information you need to understand how the 401(k) plan works in your organization and how you can contribute. Simply call your human resources department and/or see if there is information on your employer's Web site. Since 401(k) plans vary so much, you will need to confirm the details with your employer. If your employer allows you to control your 401(k) plan, then you have the freedom to direct where you want to invest your contributions. You will need to research the different funds and stocks that are available to decide how you would like to allocate your contribution. Remember, diversification is important. If you need additional guidance, consider using a financial advisor or friend to help set up your funds.

Question 60: **What are Roth IRAs, and how are they different from traditional IRAs?**

The major differences between a Roth IRA and a traditional IRA are in the way in which they are funded and in the rules governing withdrawing funds from them. Roth IRAs are funded with your income dollars *after* taxes have been withdrawn. Traditional IRAs are funded with your income dollars *before* taxes have been withdrawn. Consequently, you are not taxed on any funds that you withdraw from a Roth IRA. And you can withdraw funds from a Roth IRA at any time, regardless of your age, without incurring a penalty. With a traditional IRA, you're taxed on withdrawals. (This is not necessarily a bad thing, since your tax rate may be lower when you retire.) Also with a traditional IRA, if you withdraw funds before you reach 59½, you must pay a 10 percent penalty on the amount withdrawn. And you must start withdrawals from a traditional IRA by age 70½.

Question 61: **Are IRAs still a good investment, and how do I open one?**

IRAs are one of the few investment options left that allow your earnings to grow, tax-free, until you elect to withdraw some or all of the funds that are in your account. Generally, you should first contribute to employer-sponsored plans such as a 401(k) plan to enjoy their matching contributions before you consider opening an IRA account.

You have a choice between managed or self-directed IRA accounts. Managed IRAs have professional managers who direct the investments on your behalf. Most mutual funds–based IRAs are managed. You pay an annual fee of about 1 percent of your holdings for this service.

Self-directed IRAs are set up so that you choose and manage the investments in your account yourself. Most brokers and mutual funds offer them. They have a small annual fee (usually $50 or less per year) and most self-directed IRAs offer a wide variety of investment options for you to consider. To open an IRA account, contact your financial institution.

Question 62: **Why should I open an IRA?**

There are two reasons why you would want to open an IRA account. The first is if your company does not have a 401(k) plan. Opening a Roth IRA or regular IRA is a good alternative for saving toward retirement. Another reason is if you leave your current employer. Often people open IRAs at this time so that they can roll their 401(k) into an IRA account to avoid incurring tax penalties.

Question 63: **Can I direct where to invest the funds that are in my IRA accounts?**

Absolutely! An IRA account can offer you the flexibility to manage your own investment portfolio. However, some financial institutions offer IRA accounts that automatically manage your funds for you by choosing the areas to invest in. It is important to check with your financial institution to see what different plans are in place, and to learn and understand your options.

Question 64: **What's a Keogh plan? Am I eligible, and should I open one?**

A Keogh plan is similar to an IRA. It is a tax-deferred retirement investment plan geared toward self-employed individuals and their employees. You may be eligible for a Keogh plan even if you have a full-time job that has a different retirement plan that you are utilizing. Several different Keogh plans are available, so you need to review your options to see if you are eligible and whether or not you should open one. To find out more about this plan and help you determine whether this plan is right for you, go to *www.401kcenter.com.*

Question 65: **What are the different types of savings plans to consider?**

A good retirement plan separates savings into three categories or funds for different purposes: an emergency savings fund, a short-term savings fund, and a long-term savings fund.

The emergency fund is the most important savings category. It is created to cover income and expenses related to emergencies such as the loss of a job or unexpected medical expenses. Most financial planners will advise you to accumulate six months of income in your emergency fund. The funds should be kept in an easy-to-access account with no penalty for withdrawal.

Short-term savings funds are used for planned expenses such as a vacation or major purchases such as a car or furniture. Regular recurring contributions are essential to assure that your "nest egg" builds at a consistent rate.

Long-term funds are typically invested in equities that can provide long-term growth. Building equity in your home is a powerful way to grow your long-term savings account. Aggressive mortgage payments, handled either by increasing the amount of your monthly payment or by making extra payments, are two popular ways to increase the equity in your home and expedite paying off your house.

Chapter 7

MINIMIZING TAXES

You've heard it before. The two sure things in this world are death and taxes. It is estimated that Americans spend more than 600 billion hours each year preparing their tax returns. Given that amount of time and effort spent on this dreaded task, it is no wonder that the subject of taxes creates a lot of emotion and misconceptions. As a result, many people make poor decisions when it comes to dealing with their taxes. They wonder: Should I prepare my own tax return? How do the tax laws affect my retirement accounts? How do I minimize my tax liabilities after I retire? Although the entire topic of taxes can't be covered in a single chapter—or in an entire book, for that matter—we do address major tax issues that you should be aware of before and after you retire.

Question 66: **How does the Tax Relief Act of 1997 affect me?**

In 1997 Congress passed an IRS reform bill, which makes it much easier for the average taxpayer to receive fair treatment under the tax laws. Under the law, known as the Tax Relief Act of 1997, the burden of tax-fraud proof is the responsibility of the government instead of the taxpayer. Prior to this law, mistreated taxpayers could not sue the IRS for damages. Now, with the passing of the law, they can.

The law expanded eligibility for traditional IRAs and created the Roth IRA and new education IRAs to help pay college expenses for your children. The Roth IRA is a variation of the traditional IRA. While maximum contribution levels to a Roth IRA are the same as for a regular IRA (i.e., $4,000 or $5,000 per person per year depending on age), tax treatment and eligibility are much different. Your contributions to a Roth are not tax-deductible, but your withdrawals are tax-free as long as the account has been open at least five years and the withdrawals are made after age 59½.

Your income level is the sole determining factor for Roth IRA eligibility. To contribute the full amount per year per individual, your adjusted gross income must be $99,000 or less for single taxpayers and $156,000 or less for joint filers (in 2007). The new Roth option can give you a reason to re-evaluate your retirement strategy. Is it better to pay taxes now and avoid paying them later or is it better to defer taxes now? The answer depends on your present and future financial situation.

Question 67: **Should I hire an accountant to do my taxes?**

Someone might opt to use an accountant over doing their own taxes for a variety of reasons. Some people feel more comfortable having a professional reviewing their taxes. Another reason is to utilize the professional's expertise in hopes of finding potential tax breaks and cost-saving strategies based on the individual's situation. Finally, people who have more complex tax returns often prefer having accountants do the job. It will cost you money to use an accountant, and you have to decide if you would feel more comfortable using an accountant or if you are fine with doing it yourself.

Question 68: **What are the benefits of doing my own taxes?**

You can save time and money by doing your own taxes. Consider using some of the great tax-preparation software on the market that will walk you through the process. Tax-preparation software is, in our opinion, one of the best applications ever created for the personal computer. It virtually does away with tedious calculations, helps eliminate math errors, and automatically produces the tax forms you need to complete your return. That last feature in and of itself makes the software purchase worthwhile.

Most of the user-friendly tax software walks you through a series of questions about your tax return and calculates the final information based upon your responses to the questions. When you are done, the application provides you with official, completed tax-return forms that are ready for submission. It will even ask you if you want it to file your return electronically, which expedites the process. And you get all this for about $30 to $50 for the federal tax software and about $10 for your state tax software. It's an amazing deal when you think about it. One of the better software applications available is TurboTax by Intuit Corporation. You can get more information and compare their tax products on their Web site at *www.turbotax.intuit.com.*

Question 69: **Can I withdraw funds from a retirement account before I am 59½ without incurring a tax penalty?**

Unfortunately, the answer is no. Even though the money is yours, if you withdraw any from your account prior to turning 59½, the money will be subject to income taxes based on your current salary bracket and tax rate. There is also a mandatory 20 percent tax withholding deposit that is applied up front to the money being withdrawn. Not only will you face tax penalties, but you will also experience an early-withdrawal penalty, which is around 10 percent. Certain hardship exceptions are available for individuals in need, so if you get in a serious bind, consider looking into this in greater detail.

Question 70: **Can I borrow money from my retirement account?**

Most plans allow you to borrow up to 50 percent of what you have in your plan. If you need to borrow money, use this option only as a last resort. If you borrow from your plan and, for whatever reason, you can't pay it back, the money will come out of your plan to pay the loan. You'll be required to pay income tax on the withdrawal and the IRS will charge you a 10 percent early-withdrawal penalty.

Question 71: **What are annuities, how do they work, and what are the tax advantages?**

Annuities are hybrid products that combine the advantages of long-term investments with the advantages of life insurance. They are sold like securities by insurance companies. They differ from insurance policies, where you typically pay monthly premiums. With an annuity, you pay a lump sum up front to guarantee a periodic payout immediately or starting at some future date that you choose. Annuity payments continue for as long as you live.

Fortunately, people are living longer, which can pose a quandary for those who are worried about outliving their savings. One way to save for retirement and ensure that your money lasts as long as you do is to invest in an annuity. Annuities come in two basic categories: deferred and immediate-income annuities.

A deferred annuity allows you to save money for retirement on a tax-deferred basis until you start withdrawing money from the account. You can choose between a fixed or variable tax-deferred annuity. The variable option allows you to withdraw money from your annuity at whatever amount fits your needs. A fixed annuity allows you to convert your annuity into a "fixed" monthly source of income over your lifetime. The monthly amount is dependent upon your age when you initiate the conversion.

An immediate-income annuity is a contract issued to you by an insurance company that turns a single lump-sum payment into payments (i.e., monthly) over your lifetime or, if you prefer, for a specific number of years. Most annuities offer payment features that cover your spouse after you die. You can opt to receive full or reduced joint income, depending on your situation. Most major life insurance companies offer a variety of annuity products. Web sites such as *www.annuityshopper.com* offer annuity quotes based on your age and other criteria.

Question 72: **What are the advantages and disadvantages of annuities?**

Advantages:

- They offer a guaranteed payment amount that's locked in. Although the timing of the payments might vary, depending upon the type of annuity you've selected, the guarantee makes retirement planning easier.
- They offer insurance in case you outlive your savings. Most annuities offer you a guaranteed payment for life.
- They offer you tax-deferred income. Annuity income is taxed only when you elect to receive it. Your tax rate is usually lower after you retire.

Disadvantages:

- You'll pay relatively high sales fees when you purchase an annuity. Don't forget that a portion of the purchase price of your annuity goes toward a life insurance policy on you.
- Only a portion of the purchase price goes toward investments.
- If you die early, you won't get the full potential of your annuity payout.
- Most annuities offer a fixed monthly payout that is not adjusted for inflation.

Chapter 8

UNDERSTANDING SOCIAL SECURITY

Despite the spreading fear that social security will fold, be aware that social security is here for the long term. True, the program needs financial bolstering to ensure that there will be sufficient money to cover the surge of baby boomers who are about to tap into the system, but the political consequences of a social security disaster will ensure its survival. So, disregard the rhetoric and start analyzing the benefit you'll get to supplement your retirement income.

Question 73: **How much social security income can I count on in retirement?**

As a general rule, social security will cover about 25 percent of your pre-retirement income (less if you're rich; more if you're poor). Social security uses a formula to calculate what is called your Average Indexed Monthly Earnings (AIME) at retirement. Currently, your payment is based on 90 percent of the first $592 of your monthly income, 32 percent of the next $2,975, and then 15 percent of the amount over $3,567. The maximum monthly benefit you can receive at age 65 is $1,874 per month.

Your social security income is tax-free unless you are married and your annual earnings are more than $32,000 or single with earnings exceeding $25,000, which includes half of your social security income in that total. The percentage of your social security that's taxable grows as your adjusted gross income grows. A maximum of 85 percent will be taxable if your adjusted annual income on a joint return reaches $44,000 ($35,000 for singles).

Question 74: **What do I need to be aware of regarding social security?**

Carefully plan your absences from the work force. If you decide to take time off, be aware that the time you are not working counts against you when your social security benefit is calculated. If you decide to leave your full-time job, consider working part time to earn money that will count toward your retirement benefit.

If you earn less than your spouse, consider taking your benefit at age 62. The spousal benefit is almost always larger if the lower-earning spouse had consistently low earnings over a short work life, while the other spouse is on track for maximum benefits.

If you are divorced, protect your right to benefits based on your ex-spouse's earnings. You're entitled to social security checks calculated according to your ex-spouse's work history if one-half of their benefit is larger than what you would have received based on your own work history.

Call the Social Security Administration (800-772-1213) and ask them to send you form SSA-7004 for your personal earnings and benefits estimate. Start checking their records against your annual W-2 forms to make sure that your benefit earning potential is accurately recorded.

Question 75: **Am I eligible for social security benefits?**

If you have worked for ten or more years and were born in or after 1929, then you are eligible for retirement benefits through social security. The official Web site for social security has a great tool called the Benefit Eligibility Screening Tool (BEST) that can help you identify which of the different social security programs you may be eligible for. The BEST can be found by going to *www.ssa.gov*. This is a great starting point for understanding your retirement benefits and qualifications.

Question 76: **How do delayed retirement credits work?**

Many individuals decide to retire after 65 years of age. For this reason, social security provides credit to individuals delaying their retirements by increasing the monthly percentage of social security that they will collect once they retire. For example, if you were born between 1933 and 1934, your yearly rate of increase is 5.5 percent and your monthly rate of increase is 11/24 of 1 percent. To find out what rate increase you would receive, go to *www.ssa.gov/retire2/delayret.htm*. The benefit increase will not apply after you reach the age of 70, even if you decide to delay your benefits. Therefore you should make sure to apply for social security prior to your seventieth birthday.

Question 77: **When can I retire with social security?**

Your "full retirement age" depends on what year you were born. Depending on your birth year, your full retirement age is anywhere between 65 and 67. To calculate your specific retirement age, go to *www.ssa.gov/pubs/ageincrease.htm*. As mentioned in the previous question, if you decide to retire past your full retirement age, you still qualify for retirement benefits. If you are interested in taking advantage of your social security benefits before that age, you can do so as early as 62 years of age. However, if you opt to begin your plan early, be aware that you will receive a decrease in your monthly social security checks because the program takes into account your age. To better understand the age 62 reduction amounts, review the chart at *www.ssa.gov/retire2/agereduction.htm.*

Question 78: **How does my retirement age affect my benefits?**

Your age and earning level are what determines the amount of social security you are able to collect. You can get a quick estimate of your potential benefit amounts through an online calculator found at *www.ssa.gov/planners/calculators.htm.* The calculator is strictly a reference tool to help you determine when you want to retire and help you plan your retirement based on the estimated benefits you may receive.

Question 79: **How do my retirement benefits work if I get a divorce?**

In a nutshell, if you were married for at least ten years and decide to get a divorce, you may be able to collect retirement benefits on your former spouse's social security record. There are certain criteria that you need to be aware of to help determine if you qualify:

1. You must be at least 62 years old.
2. You must be unmarried.
3. You must not be eligible for an equal or higher benefit on your own social security record, or on someone else's social security record.

To find out more specifics, you can go to *www.ssa.gov/retire2/yourdivspouse.htm.*

Question 80: **Can I work after I retire and still collect on social security?**

Yes. In fact, many people do. Once you reach full retirement age (see question 77), there is no limit on the amount you can earn while collecting social security benefits. However, if you decide to work prior to reaching full retirement age and still collect social security, then you should be aware of the following impacts to your benefits:

1. If you are under full retirement age, $1 will be deducted from your benefit payments for every $2 you earn above the annual limit.
2. When you reach full retirement age, $1 will be deducted for every $3 earned above a different limit, but it is only counted toward earnings from the month before you reach full retirement age.
3. Starting with the month you reach full retirement age, you can get benefits with no limit on your earnings. For example, if you were born in 1940, your full retirement age is 65 years and 6 months so you can begin to collect with no limit at 65½ years old.

If you are interested in getting additional information, visit *www.ssa.gov/retire2/whileworking.htm*.

Question 81: **When does my Medicare start?**

Medicare goes into effect at the age of 65. If you are collecting social security at full retirement age, then your Medicare hospital benefits start automatically. However, if you are 65 and have not begun to collect social security, you should still sign up for Medicare at the age of 65 to avoid any increases in pricing. There is a list of things that you will need to supply to the Social Security offices when signing up for Medicare. You can go to *www.ssa.gov/online/ssa-1.html* to learn more.

Question 82: **Will Medicare be deducted from my social security benefits?**

If you elect Medicare's Supplementary Insurance (Part B), which helps to pay doctor bills, the premium will be deducted from your social security check.

Question 83: **What does Medicare cover and not cover?**

Medicare coverage comes in two parts. Part A covers hospital bills and bills from skilled nursing homes, hospice care, and a certain amount of home health care. You pay for this coverage through your social security taxes and are automatically covered beginning at age 65.

Part B is optional and covers doctor bills, outpatient surgery, emergency room treatment, X-rays, laboratory tests, a portion of prescription drugs, and medical equipment such as wheelchairs. When you register for Part A, you will be asked if you want to participate in Part B. The answer should be "yes" unless you have an excellent private insurance policy that covers Part B expenses. A monthly premium for Part B gets deducted from your social security check. However, there are three primary fees that are not covered by Medicare:

- You will pay an up-front deductible fee every time you are hospitalized.
- If you are hospitalized for over ninety days, you will have to pay a daily deductible fee for every day past the ninety-day mark.
- Medicare pays 80 percent of physician fees and other medical services. However, you will be responsible for paying the other 20 percent.

Question 84: **Can I leave the United States and still collect on my benefits?**

If you are a United States citizen, then you can freely travel or live in most foreign countries without impact to your social security benefits. If you are actually living in a foreign country, you may be able to get payments directly to your foreign address. However, the list of qualifying countries changes daily, so it's important to read more about your place of residency and how your social security benefits work. If you are within the United States, you can call 800-772-1213 for more information. If you are outside of the Unites States, you can reference *www.ssa.gov/pubs/10137.html* to get the number of the office in your area or to read more about your country.

Question 85: **What do I do to start receiving social security benefits when I become eligible?**

The government does not automatically enroll anyone in social security, so you have to contact them and complete the necessary applications. The following question tells you more about the application process.

Question 86: **How do I apply for social security?**

You apply for social security three months before you want your benefits to start. When you apply, you will need to submit a completed form, as well as a certified copy of your birth certificate. You can apply online at *www.ssa.gov*, by mail (forms are online), or over the phone at 800-772-1213.

Question 87: **My situation has changed, so how do I change my social security records?**

All changes can be reported by calling the main number at 800-772-1213. Typical changes include a new address, new marital status, or returning to work if you were under disability benefits.

Question 88: **Once I'm on social security, how much am I allowed to earn without incurring a reduction in my social security payment?**

The answer to this question depends on the individual. You can get your personalized answer by going to the Social Security Administration's Web site at *www.ssa.gov/retire2/whileworking.htm*. The site provides you with a calculator that will help you in determining your maximum earning potential without incurring a reduction in your monthly social security payment. If you're under "full retirement age," the most you can earn in 2007 without incurring a reduction is $12,960.

PART II

Investing in Your Retirement Income

Chapter 9

GETTING STARTED

If you want to be successful at supplementing your retirement income, you must have a framework on which to hang all of your thoughts about ways to increase your income. Should you buy a mutual fund or that hot stock that your golf buddy told you about? How do you choose between stocks and bonds? Should you look into investing in real estate or starting a personal business?

There are logical answers to these questions, but only if you start with a sensible investment plan. Once you've created that plan, the direction that you should take will become clearer. You'll know exactly what kinds of investments to make.

Question 89: **Why is investing considered a critical part of a retirement plan?**

You want your hard-earned money to continue to grow and prosper. To do that, you need to begin building an investment portfolio that encompasses your goals, risk tolerance, and time horizon. Your ultimate financial goal may be to retire in style. How soon you retire, and in what style, can significantly affect your decisions on how you allocate your assets. How you choose to diversify (e.g., stocks, bonds, mutual funds) depends on the following:

- Your rate-of-return goals
- How much risk you can tolerate
- How long you can invest your capital
- Your personal tax liability
- Your need for quick access to cash

Question 90: How do I determine the level of investment risk that I'm comfortable with?

If you have a high tolerance for volatility, you may want to invest as much as 70 percent of your holdings in the stock market, 25 percent in bonds, and only 5 percent in a money market account. If you have less stomach for volatility, you may want to keep 50 percent in stocks or mutual funds, 40 percent in bonds, and the rest in money market accounts.

Question 91: Why is it important to diversify my investments?

Before you start investing in anything, make sure you know how diversified you are in what you already own. This is important because diversifying your accounts keeps your portfolio in balance. Many investors may not know if their investments are diversified because the mutual funds and stocks that they own are in their 401(k) and retirement plans. If this applies to you, find out exactly what you plan to invest in. For example, some funds call themselves small-cap. But, given the less-than-stellar performance of large-cap stocks over the past few years, these same funds may have veered off into small-cap territory to boost their returns. It's your duty to understand where your money is invested, so make sure you get this information and review it. Without this knowledge, you could be under the false assumption that your stocks are diversified across companies.

Question 92: How do I establish my investment goals and objectives?

To establish your goals and objectives for any investment planning, you will need to conduct a financial analysis of your current investment positions. If you have already done this, then you are off to a good start. Your goals should include preservation and appreciation of principle and the generation of a stable after-tax income. Your objectives will be derived from your goals and will help you to determine your future financial state based on your desired standard of living.

Question 93: What are the basic types of investments that I should consider?

Money magazine's Web site has a feature that is called Money 101. Lesson 4 (found at *http://money.cnn.com/pf/101/lessons/4/*) walks you through the basics of investment types and what you need to know. Stocks, bonds, notes, and funds are just a few of the types of investments that are covered. This site is a great place to start to understand your different investment options and what to look out for. You will need to review each investment option in detail to help you determine the right strategy for you.

Question 94: What should I consider when I build my portfolio?

Here's an overview of important points you should consider when building your portfolio:

- *Is time on your side?* Investors with more years until retirement can afford to put a greater percentage of their assets in the stock market. If time is not on your side, you may want to consider conservative mutual funds or bonds.
- *Stocks mean risk with higher returns.* Investors with a higher tolerance for volatility should put more money in the stock market than those who have a lower tolerance for risk.

- *Get professional advice.* One of the best ways to build a solid portfolio is to periodically consult a qualified broker or knowledgeable friend for advice and ideas.
- *Make diversification a key goal.* Studies show that asset diversification is the single most important factor in determining solid returns from both short- and long-term investments.

Question 95: How often should I revise my investment plan?

As a rule of thumb, revise your investment plan as soon as things change (the economy, your personal life, etc.). In fact, if you don't do it at least once every six months, you are probably not monitoring your investments as you should. Diversify your portfolio across different industries and sectors. For example, you may decide to invest in five to ten stocks from different industries and never let any one be more than 20 percent of your total portfolio. If there is a sudden downturn in the economy, it may be appropriate to pull your money out of the market and put it into a money market account until things get better.

Question 96: What is a watch list?

A watch list is a listing of stocks and mutual funds that are, for whatever reason, of interest to you. A typical watch list includes the name and trade symbol of the equity you're "watching," the share price on the day you incorporated it into your list, and a brief reason why you added it to your list (e.g., recommendation from friend, magazine article, etc.). The purpose of the list is to watch specific stocks or funds over some period of time to determine how they perform in the market, before you invest in them.

Question 97: **How do I set up and use a watch list?**

Almost every financial organization, as well as many Internet brokers, offer their clients the option to create a watch list online through their Web sites. This list is a way for you to monitor potential investments and personalize it based on your investments strategies. You can create a watch list manually on a piece of paper if you don't have access to one on the Internet. Either way, it is an effective way to monitor your investments.

Question 98: **What's a portfolio?**

Similar to a watch list, a portfolio is a listing of stocks and mutual funds that you actually own. A typical portfolio includes the name and trade symbol of the equity you own, the number of shares, the price per share that you paid on the day you incorporated it into your portfolio, and a brief reason why you bought it. The purpose of a portfolio is to help you track the performance of stocks or funds you own to determine how they are performing in the market.

Question 99: **How do I set up and use a portfolio?**

A portfolio is usually set up online so it can be updated easily. Every brokerage organization, including Internet brokers, offers their clients the option to create a portfolio online using their Web sites. Many offer this feature as part of their customer service. You can reference *www.ehow.com* to get a simple list of things you need to do in order to set up and use a portfolio.

Question 100: **What are five "easy-to-follow" information sources that will keep me informed about what's happening in the investment world?**

Some of the top financial information sources that are easy to navigate are:

- Charles Schwab at *www.schwab.com*
- *Investor's Business Daily* at *www.investors.com*
- *Money* magazine at *www.money.cnn.com*
- Yahoo Financial at *www.finance.yahoo.com*
- *Financial News* at *www.financialnews-us.com*

Question 101: **How can I defend my portfolio against major losses?**

There is a stock sell feature that is worth reviewing; it is called a stop loss. What this allows you to do is to put in a sell order if the stock you purchased drops to a certain price. Generally speaking, you typically would consider a stop loss of 10 percent less than your purchase price. For example, if you buy a stock at $100 a share, you may want to subsequently put in a stop loss order through your broker for $90. This means that if the stock you purchased goes down to $90, you are putting in the order to have the stock sold for you. You would experience a loss of $10 a share, but you are also protecting yourself against a major loss so that if it drops dramatically (i.e., more than 10 percent), you did not absorb additional losses on the stock. A stop loss also gives you the freedom of not having to monitor a stock as closely as you would without it because the sell is automated. For additional information about the stop loss feature, go to *www.schwab.com* and search for stop loss.

Question 102: **I have $10,000 to invest. What's the next step?**

Your next step is to research the best investment for you based on your age, risk assessment, strategies, goals, and objectives. There are equations you can use that help you determine where best to put your money based on the criteria we mentioned. You can go to *www.money.cnn.com* for their Investment 101 training sessions that are conducted online.

Question 103: What is dollar cost averaging?

Dollar cost averaging is a strategy of buying securities (typically mutual funds and stocks) in fixed dollar amounts at scheduled intervals, with the aim being to lower the average cost per share over time. Please be aware that dollar cost averaging does not assure a profit and does not protect against loss in declining markets.

Question 104: How much of my income should I save?

The typical rule of thumb is to save at least 10 percent of your salary. If you can afford to save at least this amount, then you're doing great. Many other saving plans reference an 80-to-20-percent plan. This means that you spend 80 percent of your income and save 20 percent. If you are following this model, you are on track for a healthy savings toward your retirement.

Chapter 10

INVESTING IN MUTUAL AND EXCHANGE-TRADED FUNDS

The secret to investing in mutual funds and Exchange-Traded Funds (ETFs) is simplicity. Wall Street is constantly urging buyers to purchase this and buy that. However, chances are that the more complicated the fund is, the riskier it is. "Flashy" funds almost always profit the vendors selling them more than they profit you.

You don't need to own complicated funds. You can rack up a superb retirement nest egg with just three or four good stock-owning mutual funds, maybe a bond fund and an ETF. The questions and subsequent answers in this chapter will help you simplify your investment plan.

Question 105: What are mutual funds?

A mutual fund is an open-ended fund operated by an investment company that raises money from shareholders and invests in one lump investment (i.e., the fund) that typically has a common investment objective. The investment objectives between funds can vary widely, with some investing in small-cap companies and others in large-cap companies. Mutual funds offer investors the opportunity to pool their money together and buy into multiple stocks, bonds, and real estate. Choosing the right mutual funds offers a way for you to diversify your investments and reap the benefits of a nice return on your money.

Question 106: **What are the advantages of investing in mutual funds?**

Most funds offer the benefit of allowing you to deposit a certain amount each month into the fund to increase the number of shares you own. By spreading your investment out over time, you develop a consistent savings plan within your investment plan. Here are several advantages of owning mutual funds:

- **Diversification.** When you invest in a fund, your money is riding on a large number of securities instead of just a few, which minimizes the risk.
- **Low-cost management.** Professional management fees typically run about 1 percent of your investment annually.
- **Liquidity.** You can sell your mutual funds any time, just like stocks.
- **Flexibility.** If you've invested in one of the funds such as Fidelity Investments's family of funds, you can switch between the different funds in the family as market conditions dictate or your investment objectives change.

Question 107: **How do I find a good mutual fund?**

There are more than 800 mutual funds to choose from, so choosing the right fund for yourself can be tedious. Here's how to quickly go about finding the better funds:

- Read up. A number of books out there specialize in investing in funds. *Morningstar Guide to Mutual Funds: Five-Star Strategies for Success* by Christine Benz gives you a quick roundup of investment tips.
- Use research tools. *Barron's* magazine and the *Wall Street Journal* publish fund performance data.
- Use the Internet. *www.morningstar.com*, *www.kiplinger.com*, and *www.investools.com* are three sites to start with.
- Check the ads. Don't ignore the ads in newspapers and financial magazines. Fund companies like to advertise their better-performing funds.

Question 108: **What are the different types of mutual funds?**

Because there are so many different funds, we have put together this chart to help simplify the fund type, risk level, investment type, and objective for you to review:

Mutual Funds by Type and Risk Level

Fund Type	Risk Level	Investment Types	Objective
Money market	Low	Commercial paper such as CDs and Treasury notes	Earn short-term interest rates from secure investments
Tax-exempt money market	Low	Short-term municipal bonds	Earn short-term tax-exempt interest
International money market	Medium low	Foreign CDs and other foreign securities	Get higher returns than U.S. CDs and securities
Short-term and intermediate bonds	Medium low	Government and corporate bonds with expiration terms of less than 10 years	Safe capital investments at rates that are higher than the money market

Fund Type	Risk Level	Investment Types	Objective
Long-term bonds	Medium	Government and corporate bonds with mature dates between 15 and 30 years	Speculate on low interest rates to get higher returns
International bonds	Medium	Bonds from foreign companies and countries	Get higher return than on comparable U.S. bonds
Income securities	Medium	Bonds and dividend-producing stocks	Income with diversification
Equity income	Medium high	Blue chip stocks that pay high dividends	Modest income combined with good growth
Growth and income	Medium high	Stocks with high dividends and growth	More emphasis on growth than income
Asset allocation	Medium high	Constantly changing portfolio mix to take advantage of the market at any one time	Emphasis on growth while limiting losses in any market
Stock index	Medium high	Stocks that match the performance of a specific market	Achieve the average market return
Large company	Medium high	Stock in large companies	Stock reliability and performance over time
Medium-size companies	High	Stock in medium-size companies	A better return than with large company stocks
Real estate	High	Stock in real estate companies	High speculative returns and a hedge against inflation
Growth	High	Stocks with fast earnings records	Earn above-average market return

Fund Type	Risk Level	Investment Types	Objective
Aggressive growth	Very high	High-growth stocks	Higher performance than most other investment options
Microcap	Very high	Very small potentially high-growth companies	Stocks that substantially outperform the market

Question 109: **If I decide to invest in mutual funds, what brokers are available to help me?**

When you review the prospectus and portfolio of available funds of any mutual fund company, the fund's objective and risk factor will be identified in the prospectus.

If you are ready to contact a broker to help you find a suitable fund, here are four brokerage companies that are major players in the mutual fund market:

- Charles Schwab's OneSource fund group (800-435-4000)
- Fidelity's Funds Network (800-544-9697)
- Vanguard Mutual Funds (800-662-7447)
- T. Rowe Price Mutual Funds (800-638-5660)

Question 110: **How do I calculate my mutual fund fees and expenses?**

The mutual fund's fees and expenses are an important part of the decision-making process when choosing which fund to invest in. These charges can lower your return, so you want to be aware of how they work and the impact up front. To help with this, the Security and Exchange Commission has added a cost calculator on its Web Site at *www.sec.gov/investor/tools/mfcc/mfcc-intsec.htm*. If you link to *www.sec.gov/investor/tools/mfcc/mfcc-int.htm* you will be able to get the answer to this question.

Question 111: What's the difference between load and no-load mutual funds?

The difference is that when you purchase a no-load fund, you are not charged a sales fee or points when you acquire the fund. Load funds charge sales points. On the surface, no-load funds would appear to be the best choice since no one likes to pay unnescessary sales commissions or fees. However, consider whether it is worth paying a sales fee to acquire a top-grade fund that's producing the returns you want.

If you are interested in getting fund research material, consider getting one of the better resources such as Morningstar No-Load Funds newsletter (800-735-0700). It features nearly 700 no-load and low-load mutual funds monthly. Value Line (800-577-4566) is another valuable newsletter that you can try.

Question 112: How do you buy and sell mutual funds?

Typically, you can buy or sell funds directly through your fund company. However, if the funds were purchased through another source, such as a third-party broker, you can go directly to them, but you will most likely incur a sales charge. To avoid any charges, several financial organizations—e.g., Schwab's One Source, Vanguard's Fund Access, and Fidelity's Funds Network—offer no-charge options.

Question 113: What are Exchange-Traded Funds?

An ETF, like a mutual fund, is an index fund that trades in the market like a stock. Most ETFs are offered on the American Stock Exchange and cover a wide range of diverse investments. For example, if you're interested in diversifying your investment in the NASDAQ exchange, QQQQ is the trade symbol of an ETF that allows you to do that. It's made up of 100 prominent NASDAQ-traded stocks. DIA (trade symbol) is the equivalent of QQQQ that covers the primary stocks on the New York stock exchange. There are over 200 ETFs for you to consider. If you are interested in reading more about ETFs, go to *www.investopedia.com.*

Question 114: **Why have ETFs become so popular?**

ETFs have become extremely popular because owning an ETF allows you the diversification features of a mutual fund while providing the flexibility of trading like a stock. Another reason for their popularity is that ETFs offer investors a way to diversify their investments without having to pay the high premiums that many mutual funds charge. Today, there are more than 200 ETFs that you can buy that cover dozens of market sectors including leisure, semiconductors, health care, oil, precious metals, and networking.

Question 115: **What are the advantages of ETFs?**

When you invest in an ETF, you become a shareholder in a portfolio of a vast variety of stocks. You don't have to worry about the volatility of a single stock since your investment is spread across several stocks. ETFs are among the least time consuming of all investing strategies to maintain. Additional advantages of owning ETFs include:

- **Professionally managed:** A professional portfolio manager handles all buying and selling of stocks in the fund as well as all the other day-to-day responsibilities, leaving you to do other things, such as playing golf.
- **Low-cost:** Annual expenses for ETFs range between 0.1 percent and 0.65 percent versus up to 2 percent for a regular mutual fund.
- **Time-efficient:** Many investors do not wish to pore over annual reports and would prefer a more passive approach. Because of their relative diversity, ETFs are ideal for investors who lack the time or inclination to select individual stocks.

- **Flexible:** An ETF may be traded any time the exchanges are open. Open-ended mutual funds can only be redeemed at the closing price of the day.

Question 116: **What are the different types of ETFs?**

There are several types of ETFs:

- **Sector ETFs:** Sector ETFs do what their name implies; they restrict investments to a particular industry or sector of the market.
- **Index ETFs:** For many investors, index ETFs are by far the easiest, most effective way to go. If your goal is long-term growth without having to pay much attention, these workhorse funds are the best solution. They simply buy all the stocks in a chosen index (i.e., QQQQ, DIA, etc.) with the goal of matching that group's performance.
- **Blend ETFs:** These ETFs can go across the board. They might invest in both high-growth tech stocks and communication companies. Because of their mixed blends, they can be difficult to classify in terms of risk.
- **Value ETFs:** Value ETFs like to invest in companies that the market has overlooked. They search for stocks that have become "undervalued" or priced low relative to their earnings potential.
- **Growth ETFs:** As their name implies, growth ETFs tend to look for the fastest-growing companies on the market. Growth ETFs are willing to take more risk in an effort to build a portfolio of companies with above-average momentum or price appreciation.
- **Micro-cap ETFs:** These funds look for companies with market values below $250 million and tend to look for start-up companies that are about to exploit new markets. With stocks this small, the risk is always extremely high, but the growth potential is exceptional.

- **Small-cap ETFs:** A small-cap ETF focuses on companies with a market value below $1 billion. Their volatility often depends on the aggressiveness of their manager. They typically invest in hot growth companies and take high risks in hopes of high rewards.
- **Mid-cap ETFs:** These ETFs fall in the middle of the capital value range. They invest in companies with market values in the $1 to $6 billion range. The stocks at the lower end of their range are likely to exhibit the growth characteristics of smaller companies and therefore add some volatility to these funds.
- **Large-cap ETFs:** These funds focus on companies with a market value above $6 billion. Their volatility is reduced because of the size of the companies that are in their portfolios.

Question 117: What are the advantages of investing in ETFs versus individual stocks?

ETFs can minimize the risk that follows an investment in an individual stock. For example, buying into the ETF known as the NASDAQ 100 Index Tracking Stock (QQQQ) enables you to share in over 100 companies and diversifies your investment in several industries, so that losses in one are offset by gains in others. By contrast, if you put your entire investment into an individual stock, that stock could go south and take your investment with it.

Question 118: How are ETFs traded?

As with stocks, the cost or price of an ETF varies daily depending on market conditions. To determine the current price per share, you look up the daily price of a share in the ETF of your choice. Since ETFs are traded like stock, you should be aware that you can short sell, sell on margin, or purchase a certain number of shares.

Depending on your method of transaction, the price will vary throughout the market day.

You buy and sell ETFs just as you do with stock; through your broker. They can also be purchased and sold online. You simply contact your broker or buying/selling agent and initiate the transaction through her. The same commissions and restrictions apply to ETFs as they do to stocks.

Question 119: **Are ETFs a better investment alternative than mutual funds?**

ETFs are an attractive alternative to mutual funds because they trade during the day. In a nutshell, if you put in an order to sell your ETF, the transaction will go through in minutes. They also allow investors to buy shares in a portfolio of a wide variety of stocks and bonds. If you would like to read more about the benefits of buying ETFs over mutual funds, see financial advisor Suze Orman's article at *http://biz.yahoo.com/pfg/e09etf.*

Question 120: **How can I use mutual funds and ETFs to diversify my investments?**

Both mutual funds and ETFs offer the advantage of diversifying your investment portfolio based on the way these funds work. When you invest in either one, you're buying shares in a portfolio of securities managed by a professional investment firm. Investing in mutual funds and ETFs has proven extremely popular with investors who have minimal time to do their own analysis, are interested in diversification, and need the help of professional experts to choose the right companies to invest in.

Question 121: **What are the tax implications of owning funds?**

Funds can be taxed in three main ways: (1) when you sell the funds for more than you paid for them (2) when the fund yields dividend payments and/or capital gains (3) when you receive a distribution due to the profitable sell of the fund's securities. Make sure you are aware of how the fund you are considering selling is taxed (i.e., short-term or long-term capital gains) and how it will impact your current taxes.

Question 122: **Are there any funds that are tax-friendly?**

Many investors have turned to tax-friendly funds to keep Uncle Sam at arm's length. Municipal bond funds are tax-friendly because their interest is exempt from federal taxes, and sometimes state and local taxes as well. Vanguard Group has put some emphasis around this over the recent years. You can see their savvy charts that outline the tax benefits of some funds by going to *www.vanguard.com*.

Question 123: **Can I track the performance of funds on a watch list and portfolio?**

Absolutely. It is highly recommended that you follow funds that you are potentially interested in buying on your watch list. Enter the per-share price as of the date you added it to your watch list. Over time, does it appreciate to your satisfaction? Follow the returns of any fund that you invest in by using the same price-monitoring techniques that you did on your watch list. Put funds on your watch list and portfolio just as you would with stocks. It's an easy way to keep on eye on a fund and stay engaged with your mutual fund investments.

Chapter 11

INVESTING IN STOCKS AND BONDS

Over the long term, stocks can be an extremely profitable investment. Stocks offer you two key benefits as an investment. The first is real growth. Historically speaking, stocks have run 7 percentage points over inflation. Therefore, if you are looking for a long-term investment, stocks can yield a healthier return on your money than other investment opportunities. The second benefit is that stocks can provide you with income in case you need to live off your capital investments.

Bonds offer you an alternative investment to stocks. If the bears are racing through the stock market, bonds can offer you a safe haven to park your money until things get better.

Question 124: **What is a stock?**

Stock is an instrument that allows individuals to own a piece of an organization, and have a claim on that organization's assets and profits. Corporations have stock, while other business entities that are sole proprietorships or limited partnerships do not. The percentage of ownership you have in the company is in direct proportion to the quantity of shares that you purchase. For example, if a company has 10,000 outstanding shares and you purchase 1,000 shares of stock, you own 10 percent of that company. Most stocks also offer voting rights to their owners, which provides shareholders with a proportional vote at annual stockholders' meetings.

Question 125: **What are the advantages of investing in individual stocks?**

Stock offers the opportunity for individuals to take part in the ownership of a corporation in hopes of gaining equity as the stock value increases. As we have seen, many people have done extremely well in the stock market, but other individuals have lost a fortune. For example, many have enjoyed the ride with Microsoft, while others took the loss experienced with Enron. The market is volatile, and investing in stock can be lucrative if done with caution. It can make your retirement, but if you're not careful, it can break it as well.

Question 126: **What are the advantages and disadvantages of investing in stocks over bonds?**

Both stocks and bonds can be advantageous investment opportunities, but both have some red flags that you should be aware of. In difficult bear markets, bonds can provide the ballast in your portfolio. However, bonds typically generate a slower rate of return than stocks. Although stock can provide you a higher rate of return on your money, you are more susceptible to volatile and uncontrollable influences on the market. Ultimately, balancing your portfolio with stocks and bonds is a solid strategy to provide the diversity that you need.

For additional information on how to benefit from investing in bonds, go to the Bond Market Association's Web site at *www.investinginbonds.com*. If you're just starting out investing in bonds, this site will help you learn more about bonds or investment strategies.

Question 127: **How can I measure my risk tolerance for investing in stocks?**

Risk tolerance is a means for measuring your individualized willingness to take investment risks in exchange for a higher potential for return on your money. To measure the level of risk you are willing to take, it is important to understand how aggressive an investor you truly are. To determine this, you can take a risk tolerance test by going to *http://money.aol.com/investing*, going to Investing Basics, and clicking "What Kind of Investor Are You? Take the Quiz."

Question 128: **How does a stock trade execution work?**

The Security and Exchange Commission has a great Web site that outlines how the trade execution works and what you need to know. By going to *www.sec.gov/investor/pubs/tradexec.htm* you can read about the process and gain a better understanding of how it works.

Question 129: **How much does it cost to buy stocks?**

Typically, you buy stocks through a financial institution that offers brokerage services. However, be aware that full-service brokerage commissions can take a large bite out of your profits. For example, assume that you invest $10,000 in a stock and pay a $200 commission to a full-service broker for the buy order. The price of your stock must increase to $10,200 or 2 percent before you can break even, and then there will be another $200 commission fee when you sell. So technically, your stock price needs to reach $10,400 or increase in value by 4 percent to break even when you sell it in order to recoup both buy and sell commissions.

Several financial institutions offer online services that help reduce the commission rates (e.g., charge less than $10 a trade) to investors. It may behoove you to become more familiar with the process by using a full-service broker for your initial trades and then look into their online options such as the one offered at Fidelity Investments.

Question 130: **How do you open a brokerage account?**

Stock brokerage firms are basically cash-and-carry enterprises. They all require client prospects to submit an application and a minimum specified amount to open an account before you can start trading. The application process takes about two to three weeks to complete.

When you place an order, your broker withdraws money from your cash account to cover the trade. If you sell stock or receive a dividend, the broker adds that money to your cash account. If you develop a good history, your broker may allow you to place trades without funds in your cash account if you settle the deficit within a few days. However, be aware that nearly all brokerages include disclaimers in their application forms that make you responsible for whatever you instruct them to do on your behalf, whether verbally or in writing.

Question 131: **How can I find a good stockbroker, and what characteristics should I look for?**

Commission structures change radically between brokerage firms, depending on the wide variety of special features they may offer. When deciding which broker is best for you, factor in the features that are important to you. Here's how to find a good broker:

- *Get recommendations from friends and associates.* What brokers are they using? What do they like and dislike about their brokers? Select a reputable firm that has a good track record.

- *Conduct interviews with brokers that interest you.* Make sure you are providing them with accurate information on your investment goals so that you get the best recommendations for your needs.
- *During the personal interview, ask for names of satisfied clients they have worked with over the past two years.* Talk to other clients of the brokerage. If the brokerage has no references for you, then you may have uncovered a problem. If a broker has many highly satisfied clients, then at least one of them should be willing to talk to you on the brokerage's behalf. Also, don't hesitate to ask for your broker's credentials.
- *Make sure you understand and are comfortable with your broker's commission structure, any annual fees, transaction costs, and any other expenses that you could incur.* Find out what "free" information the brokerage firm will send you—research reports, company announcements, annual reports, Web access details, etc.

If all of this sounds like a huge time investment, you're correct. A good broker can make you financially independent. Conversely, a bad one can cause you a lot of financial damage.

Question 132: **How many stocks should I own at any one time?**

There is no right or wrong answer as to how many stocks you should own. However, as we have mentioned throughout this book, you want to make sure your portfolio is diversified, and we caution you against investing all of your money into stocks alone. With this in mind, you can get a better idea of the amount of stock you should own once you determine your investment strategy and develop your portfolio. You also want to make sure that your portfolio is manageable for you, so limit the amount of stocks you own based on your comfort level. It is always a good idea to have a financial advisor go over your portfolio and help you determine the best balancing techniques for diversification.

Question 133: **How do I pick a good stock to buy?**

Selecting a good stock is a skill in and of itself. However, some excellent tools and resources are available to help you find stocks that are considered worth buying. For starters, if you want to learn more about what it takes to pick winning stocks, then pick up a copy of Peter Lynch's book, *One Up on Wall Street* for a fascinating peek into the mind of one of the best stock pickers. If you're new to stock investing, get a copy of *Value Investing for Dummies* by Peter Sander.

Question 134: **How do a company's earnings impact the stock price?**

Earnings growth is the single most important indicator of a stock's potential to make a big jump in price (either up or down). Earnings or profits are what a company makes after paying all its obligations. When companies conclude their fiscal quarters, they announce their earnings results to the market. The companies with the best earnings growth will typically reflect this in their stock's price. Generally their stock will be up. If earnings are down, a stock will typically be down.

Question 135: **How does a stock's price-earnings ratio impact the stock's value?**

The higher a stock's price-earnings (PE) ratio, the more you stand to lose if its earnings suddenly deteriorate. What's a PE ratio? Basically, it is the total value of all the company's issued stock divided by its annual earnings (i.e., profit). For example, if XYZ Corporation has $100 million in stock issued and its earning are $1 million annually, then it would have a PE ratio of 100 (100M/1M = 100). What that number tells you is that if you bought 100 percent of XYZ's stock, it would take you 100 years to break even on your original $100 million investment, based upon XYZ's average annual earnings. Does XYZ's stock sound like a good investment to you?

Many of us saw a number of high-tech stocks that were trading at PE ratios in excess of 100 in the late 1990s go on to crash in 2000. Exorbitantly high PEs of certain stocks (e.g., tech stocks) in the late 1990s led to the meltdown of the market in early 2000 through 2003. Most astute stock investors will tell you that they avoid stocks with PEs that are greater than 20.

Question 136: **My friend is telling me about a stock that's making tons of money. Should I take my friend's advice and buy the stock?**

Don't chase hot trends. Be skeptical of a friend's advice when his recommendation does not include specific information as to why you should buy the stock. This sort of buying behavior is extremely risky. Develop your own strategies and your own system for following potentially attractive stocks. In the end, there is one fact on which all the experts agree: over time, the price of quality stocks always moves up. A good reference to review and analyze stock is *www.stat-usa.gov*. This site is sponsored by the U.S. Department of Commerce and provides financial information, economic news, indicators, and statistics that affect stocks.

Question 137: **What are the advantages and disadvantages of trading online?**

In Burton Malkiel's classic book, *A Random Walk Down Wall Street*, he debunks virtually every popular theory of stock selection employed by the gurus of Wall Street. Malkiel and his dart-throwing chimp theory caused much controversy. He contended that a blindfolded chimpanzee throwing darts at the *Wall Street Journal* could select a portfolio that would do as well as one carefully selected by the Wall Street experts. Needless to say, Malkiel was not very popular on Wall Street.

A successful stockbroker has a hundred or more clients. If that broker were to call each of her clients during the trading day and apprise them of what was happening in the market, she could only spend about four minutes per client! If the market is in a sudden downturn or upturn, your chances of getting through to your broker are next to impossible.

As an alternative, if you log onto an online broker site, you can instantly see what's happening in the market, enter buy or sell orders, track your portfolio, transfer funds, and conduct investment research, all with the click of a mouse button. While full-service brokers charge up to a $250 commissions fee per trade, an online broker's commission can be as low as $8 for the same trade. That's a whopping 350 percent savings on commission fees. Although online brokers don't offer as many of the personal services as full-service brokers, most do offer online research tools to help you get whatever information you might need to make intelligent investment decisions.

Question 138: **How do I find a good online brokerage firm?**

Word of mouth counts for a lot when it comes to selecting an online brokerage firm. Ask your friends who are actively trading stocks which firm they're using and if they like them. Also, when considering an online broker, it's important to look beyond commissions. Get answers to questions such as:

- *What research services do they offer?* Many brokers offer excellent stock research tools on their Web sites and by mail (e.g., monthly newsletters). The better the tools, the more you're likely to pay in commissions.
- *What investments can you buy?* Some brokers aren't set up to allow you to buy certain types of investments, such as mutual funds and bonds. Make sure you know what your investment options are.
- *What response do you receive when you call them?* Do you get a message saying; "Please hold for the next available representative?" How long do you have to hold? When you talk

to one of their representatives, is he knowledgeable, and does he answer your questions to your satisfaction?

- *What commissions and other fees do they charge?* Check for hidden fees. Some brokers charge a start-up fee to open an account, or an administrative charge per trade.
- *Do they have a Web site that works for you?* A well-organized trading and research screen with safeguards built in to guard against data entry errors is a must. Do you have access to real-time quotes—i.e., are stock prices current when displayed? Some brokers provide quotes that are delayed as much as 15 minutes unless you pay extra for real-time quotes.

Question 139: **How do I find reviews of the top-rated online brokers?**

A good source to get consumer feedback on the better online brokers is at *www.consumersearch.com/www/internet/online-brokers/index.html.* They help narrow the search by outlining the best online broker, premium discount broker, best discount broker, and best online broker for novices based on the features of each broker.

Question 140: **Are stocks that pay dividends generally better than stocks that don't?**

The obvious answer is yes. If you're considering buying stock in one of two companies where one pays dividends and the other doesn't, then buy the one with dividends if everything else in your comparison analysis is the same. Dividends are cash returns paid out to stockholders at a predetermined time, typically annually or semi-annually, as a return on their investment in the company's stock. Dividend pay outs are also subject to being taxed. Companies that don't pay dividends simply reinvest what they would have paid in dividends back into the company.

Some investment analysts would argue that dividends are bad because the companies that issue them "probably" don't have anything better to do with their capital. Others assert that recognizing stockholders and meeting business needs is a sign of good management. Dividends are also a sign of profitability, since they're paid out of the profits the company makes.

Companies that are losing money will tell you that dividends aren't important. Ask their public relations officer where they're investing their cash. They probably don't know.

Question 141: **What is the case for investing in bonds?**

In difficult bear markets, bonds can provide the ballast in your portfolio to offset loses in the stock market. Basically, a bond is an agreement between the bond issuer, who is borrowing the money, and the bondholder, who is lending the money. Each bond agreement is characterized by two primary questions: How long does the bond issuer (borrower) have to repay the bondholder (lender or you)? What interest rates will the issuer pay and when will interest payments be made?

The financial strength of the issuer of a bond is a key factor in your decision to invest in a bond. Obviously, if you're lending money, the first thing you want to know is the borrower's ability to pay back your principle plus interest based on the borrower's credit history. In addition to its financial strength, the duration of the bond is critical. Usually, the more time the issuer has to repay, the higher the interest rate.

Question 142: **What are the different investment options in bonds?**

You should be aware of several options in the bond market. General obligation bonds are backed by the full taxing power of the local or state government issuing the bonds. Limited tax bonds are secured by a pledge from a specific tax or category of taxes, such as a cigarette or gasoline tax. Revenue bonds are issued to finance facilities that are expected to be self-supporting, such as toll roads and baseball parks.

Historically, state and municipal bonds have had an excellent performance record for paying out interest and principle. Even during the Great Depression of the 1930s, 98 percent of all municipalities met their bond obligations. In many cases, you can buy bonds directly from the issuing government agency to avoid stockbroker commissions.

To boost bond sales, the Treasury Department is now selling inflation-indexed savings bonds, which are also known as I bonds. All I bonds' interest rates are based on the consumer price index, and you can earn interest for up to thirty years. The earnings for I bonds fluctuate with the economy; generally, they will increase in value on a monthly basis. You can buy ten- and thirty-year inflation indexed Treasury bonds that guarantee a return that will outpace inflation. When inflation rates are low, Treasury bond payout is unlikely to beat regular savings bonds. But if inflation heats up, so will the bonds' appeal, and their interest rates will proportionately meet and even exceed the inflation rate. If you would like to learn more about this topic, consider reading the free resource called *The Savings Bonds Question and Answer Book* that's published by the Department of the Treasury, U.S. Savings Bonds Marketing Department, Washington DC 20226.

Question 143: **How does the interest rate affect bonds?**

An important factor to note about owning bonds is the standard interest rate (i.e., prime rate) that's available in the market at any given time. If the market interest rate falls, bond prices usually move higher, because the interest they are paying is worth more when compared to current lower rates. When interest rates move higher, bond prices tend to move lower.

Question 144: **What are the different types of bonds to invest in?**

Bonds tend to come in all shapes and sizes. The table on the facing page gives you an idea of what's available in the bond investment market.

Question 145: **What are the tax implications when I sell stocks or bonds?**

The trick to knowing when to sell stocks or bonds is to know the tax implications prior to the sale. For example, when you sell a stock at a profit you incur capital gains taxes, which are calculated based on the amount of time that stock was actually held. As a rule, you want to minimize taxes by recognizing the smallest gain or the largest loss possible on your income tax return. It's always important to understand the tax laws and how to make them work in your favor. Therefore, make sure to consult a tax professional when purchasing or selling stocks that may have significant tax consequences.

Type of Bond	U.S. Treasuries	Mortgage-Backed Securities	Corporate Bonds	Municipal Bonds
Issuer	Issued by the U.S. government. Treasury bonds consist of Treasury bills (mature in 13 weeks to one year), Treasury notes (mature in 2 to 10 years), and Treasury bonds (mature in 10 or more years)	A pool of individual mortgages bundled together by the Government National Mortgage Assoc. (Ginnie Mae), Federal Home Loan Mortgage Corp. (Freddie Mac), or Federal National Mortgage Assoc. (Fannie Mae)	Issued by corporations; most are issued in $1,000 increments and have maturities ranging from a few weeks up to 100 years	Issued by states, cities, and local government agencies and institutions to raise money for government-developed facilities
Risk	Considered one of the safest bonds, guaranteed by the U.S. government	Only Ginnie Maes are guaranteed and backed by the U.S. government	An investment-grade bond is relatively safe and has a high bond rating	These are generally lower risk with lower yields than most other bonds
Taxes	State- and local-tax-free but subject to federal tax	Interest is taxable	Interest is taxable	Federal-tax-free along with most state and local taxes

Chapter 12

STARTING UP A PERSONAL BUSINESS

Having a personal business is now a reality for millions of Americans. With the advent of sophisticated, yet inexpensive, office equipment such as personal computers, faxes, and copiers, just about anybody can afford to set up a business. In a Yahoo small-business survey, 72 percent of respondents ages 55 and older said they would "never be too old" to start their own businesses according to an article posted on *www.usnews.com/usnews/biztech/articles/070130/30boomerentrepreneur.htm*.

Question 146: **Why should I consider starting a personal business?**

About 80 percent of boomers claim they want to work into their retirement, according to Sara Rix, senior policy adviser at the Public Policy Institute of AARP. She says "many of them will try self-employment." Some considerations that justify starting your own business include: achieving tax benefits, utilizing the benefits of modern technology, following a lifelong dream, or realizing the desire to continue to work. At *www.entrepreneur.com*, you can research different business ideas and considerations.

Question 147: **Should I consider supplementing my retirement income with income from a personal business?**

If there is a business that you've wanted to start, retirement is a good time to consider it. However, be cautious. Many businesses have significant start-up costs associated with them and require a time commitment of sixty to eighty hours per week to break even in that critical first year. If your business centers around contracting out your services, then you may be able to minimize your costs and be very profitable by taking this approach. Look at the type of work you did before retirement. Can you do that on a contract or freelance basis? If so, that may be your best option for a post-retirement business.

Question 148: **Where can I find more information about how to start a personal business?**

There are some fantastic resources available to you. The Small Business Administration (SBA) has a wonderful Web site that features articles and related information on starting a business. Simply click on *www.sba.gov* for more information. The SBA also provides links to additional resources at the bottom of their home page.

Also consider reading Daryl Allen Hall's book, *1101 Businesses You Can Start from Home*, which has several business ideas as well as information on how to implement them.

Question 149: What are the five basic steps I need to go through to set up a personal business?

1. **Open a separate business bank account.** This is a vital step because you want to separate your business transactions from your personal transactions for accounting and tax purposes.
2. **Get a vendor number from your state.** This entitles you to buy products and services wholesale from a number of wholesale outlets across the country.
3. **Set up your business to accept Visa and MasterCard.** Check with your local commercial banks to find out what you need to do to apply for a card payment system.
4. **Take full advantage of tax-deferred retirement plans such as Keogh and SEP plans.** These plans are only available to the self-employed, and in most cases, offer superior features that are not available in traditional IRA plans.
5. **Get a good accountant.** Accountants can show you how to structure your business and keep good records so that you can save thousands of dollars on legitimate tax deductions—and lessen your chances of a costly audit.

Question 150: What are the most common mistakes people make when they start a personal business?

There are several start-up mistakes that you want to avoid at all costs. We have listed some of the more common mistakes made by business owners below:

- **Mistake #1: Thinking you don't need contracts.** Not relying on written contracts is a common mistake. They can help you avoid costly misunderstandings with your customers. Let them know in advance, and in writing, what you will deliver, your payment terms, and the specifics of any warranties that you may have.
- **Mistake #2: Thinking customers will find you.** Maybe that was true in the past, but it's not anymore. In today's

competitive environment, any business that doesn't have a constant flow of new customers is probably shrinking. Be a constant advocate for your business: network, advertise, and ask for referrals.

- **Mistake #3: Thinking customers will always come back.** It takes more than a good deal to retain a customer. You'll find that your most loyal customers keep coming back because they like doing business with you. Constantly earn their business and don't ever assume that they will automatically come back.
- **Mistake #4: Not digging in during tough times.** Tough times are good times to get noticed. At the first hint of a bad economy, many small businesses panic and run for cover. They'll slash their advertising and sales budgets while they sit out the downturn. As your competitors make themselves invisible, grab the chance to stand out and be noticed with superior products and services.
- **Mistake #5: Not advertising.** Businesses that advertise almost always take market share away from businesses that don't. Tough times may be the best time to launch an advertising blitz to gain market share. You'll have the field all to yourself.
- **Mistake #6: Not networking.** Become active in local groups and associations. Look for opportunities to publicize yourself by giving speeches at civic or professional meetings. Write articles for trade magazines or offer your expertise to journalists who cover your field. All of these activities will help you find customers and build credibility with the ones you already have.

Question 151: **If I start my own business, what do I need to know about self-employed health insurance?**

With the growing desire among baby boomers to start their own businesses, the issue of individualized health insurance coverage becomes critical. Many aging entrepreneurs are without health insurance. In fact, of the 27 million working people in the United States who are uninsured, 63 percent are either self-employed or work for small businesses, according to the *www.seniorliving.about.com* article "Starting Your Own Business? Don't Forget Self-Employed Health Insurance." The article goes on to point out that in 2002, 5.6 million workers aged 50 and above were self-employed, and many of them were uninsured. When starting your own business, you want to make sure your health care is covered, whether by an individual policy, a policy obtained through your own business, your spouse's health care plan, or, if you are 65 or older, Medicare.

Question 152: **What is a franchise?**

A franchise is a business relationship in which the owner (or franchiser) of a business licenses a purchaser (franchisee) to operate an outlet of the business using concepts, property, trademarks, and trade names owned by the franchiser. Generally speaking, when you purchase a franchise, you get certain benefits that you wouldn't get if you started or purchased a business independently. For example, some companies will provide training, materials, assets, marketing, and research, and much more.

There are two basic types of franchises for you to consider. The first are trade-name franchises, such as Taco Bell. Franchise holders typically have the right to sell brand-name products by using their own marketing and selling techniques. The second type of franchise is referred to as a business-format franchise. The franchiser establishes a fully integrated relationship with the franchise owner by providing all marketing, operating manuals, training, and quality control standards.

Less than 5 percent of new franchises fail in their first year as compared to 40 percent of independent startups. This is due to the fact that most franchises have the financial and marketing support of a large parent company and thus have brand or name recognition in the marketplace.

Question 153: **What do I need to know if I consider opening a franchise?**

Many aging business owners are looking to franchises as a means to being their own boss. "Folks in their 50s are energetic," said David Hadler, senior vice president of the International Center for Entrepreneurial Development in an article posted on *www.entrepreneur.com/magazine/entrepreneur/2004/august/71812.html*. He goes on to say, "Perhaps they've lived the corporate life, and they're ready to try it on their own." Stuart Taylor, co-founder of Your New Career Inc., shares these tips to consider when opening a franchise:

- Examine your finances by evaluating how much money you need to live off of and how much you need to support and run the franchise.
- Consider having a partner who complements your strengths and weaknesses.
- Look to others, outside of your friends and family, for objective advice.
- Make sure you are passionate about and love what you are doing.

Question 154: **Where can I find information about national or international franchises?**

A complete directory of all national and international franchises is available in most good public libraries. Most franchises will also have a Web site that will provide you direct information on franchise opportunities for their business. For additional information, contact International Franchise Association, 1350 New York Avenue NW, Suite 900, Washington DC 20005 or call them at 202-628-8000.

Question 155: **What are the risks in running my own business?**

Starting your own business is a difficult challenge and can be extremely stressful. There are financial obligations, time commitments, stress on relationships, and many other contributing factors that can make being your own boss less appealing. On top of all that, only 39.5 percent of new businesses remain open after six years, according to the SBA's Office of Advocacy. There are a lot of dynamics that can crumble a new business and Gene Fairbrother, president of MBA Consulting Inc., outlines the five most common start-up mistakes in a *www.entrepreneur.com* article called "Whoops!"

1. Lack of an established financial routine. He points out the importance of knowing the flow of your money when running your business.
2. Not having the proper market research or utilizing any feedback that you may have received.
3. Offering small profit margins that will minimize potential for necessary revenue.
4. Not seeing beyond the day-to-day and neglecting to plan for the future. He indentifies the common mistake of only marketing when you need new business, without allowing for the time it takes to see results from your marketing efforts.
5. Not getting the right support for certain business needs, such as an accountant, lawyer, etc.

Question 156: **What resources are available to help me decide whether to start a small business?**

Deciding whether to start a small business can be a difficult decision. You have to think about your time, energy, finances, commitment, personal gains, goals, and more. Several organizations have mentoring programs to help entrepreneurs go through the decision-making process. For example, the National Association for the

Self-Employed (*www.nase.org*) offers a wide variety of benefits to their members that include financial advice, discounts on products, business strategies, and more. Another excellent resource is the Small Business Administration (*www.sba.gov*), which offers advice on starting your business, finance, management, etc.

Question 157: **If I start a successful personal business, can I convert it into a franchise?**

Absolutely! In fact, many business owners start their own businesses in hopes of being able to convert them to franchises. This is often where the BIG money can be. For example, if you start a business and decide to franchise, the franchise fees can be very profitable. There are several agencies that can help you franchise your business, such as *www.thefranchisebuilders.com*, as well as a wide variety of books that can assist you with this process. Two books that will help you get started are *Franchising for Dummies* by Dave Thomas and Michael Seid and *Franchise Bible* by Erwin Keup.

Question 158: **What are the advantages and disadvantages of converting a personal business into a franchise?**

Advantages:

- *Grow your capital:* Franchising allows the business owner to grow her equity and capital with minimal investment.
- *Expansion of business with limited liability:* Franchising offers virtually no contingent liability because the franchisee signs the lease and contracts, thus limiting the franchiser's liability.
- *Better management:* It can often be hard for business owners to obtain and retain good management. When you franchise, you have an entrepreneur who is buying the business and motivated to work hard to grow the business.

- *Frees you up with the growth tasks:* It is up to the franchisee to find a new location, train his personnel, build out his site, and get everything ready for the opening day.

Disadvantages:

- *It takes some of your time:* If you franchise your business, you are often committed to training new owners and to many other timely aspects that are part of your franchise package. However, it can also free you up so that you are not responsible for expanding your business to other sites.
- *Sound business requirements:* You are now responsible for creating all the necessary contracts, business plans, and detailed paperwork that are required for franchising your business. If you are not familiar with the process, this can be a challenge. However, you can always seek out guidance to help with this process, so it is not a deal-killer.

Question 159: **How do I know if my business is "franchisable"?**

First you should determine the credentials of your business. Answer questions such as: Does your business run smoothly? What sort of feedback or response have you received from the press and your customers? Does your business have a solid foundation to work from?

The second consideration to include in your thought process is about the uniqueness of your business. How does your business stand out from its competition? Do you have a unique marketable business? Is it easy to teach a new owner how to run your business? Are you using the right software application to run your business efficiently? Is your business profitable? Does it meet aggressive sales numbers to show its potential?

If you would like to learn more about franchising a business, see *Entrepreneur* magazine's Web site (*www.entrepreneur.com*) for related articles, valuable advice, and resources to help you with the process.

Question 160: **Should I consider buying an existing business or franchise?**

Buying an existing business or franchise is not a bad way to go. When you look into an existing business, the owner will need to provide you with the company's financial information. Generally, you will want to see their tax returns, balance sheets, income statements, and any other information that will help you to determine the profitability and investment potential of the business. If you can get all of the financial information you and your accountant need, you can make an informed purchasing decision.

Question 161: **How can I find businesses that are for sale?**

A commercial realtor can help you find existing businesses that are for sale in your area. Call a reputable real estate agency and ask for their best commercial sales agent. A good book to pick up would be *The Complete Guide to Buying a Business* by Fred Steingold and Emily Dostow. You can also begin to look at some Web sites online that have current "for sale" business listings. Here are three to help you get started:

- *www.bizbuysell.com*
- *www.businessesforsale.com*
- *www.sba.gov/hotlist/franchise.html*

PART III

Improving Your Quality of Life

Chapter **13**

FINDING GREAT TRAVEL BARGAINS

Enjoy yourself and make fun a priority during your retirement. You've worked hard and now you get to reap the benefits. Take some adventures, go beyond the ordinary, and seek out the joys of retirement. The best aspect of traveling during retirement is that you can choose the optimal time to visit popular destinations—and miss the traffic that comes with peak season vacations.

Question 162: **I've heard a lot about senior travel discounts. What are they, and are they worthwhile?**

Hotels, museums, movie theaters, and other places offer discounts to the older population. For example, if you are 62 or older, the U.S. Forest Service will offer you a lifetime pass to all the national parks for only $15. If you're a bargain hunter and like to save, then you need to step forward and admit that you deserve the senior citizen discount. You can go to *www.seniordiscounts.com* or *http://frugalliving.about.com/od/seniorcitizens* to find out more about some great discounts.

Question 163: **What are the best travel destinations and resources for seniors?**

There are several sources of information that can help you choose your next trip or hot spot to visit. If you want to make traveling top on your priority list, then consider getting a monthly subscription to a travel magazine. *Budget Travel* is an excellent travel magazine that features the latest travel bargains. It provides budget-saving solutions to anywhere you may want to go. There's a section that lists the special deals that are going on each month with related Web links and contacts to get more information.

There is a fantastic site that can help you find your next destination. Just go to *http://travel.discovery.com*. This Web site has a listing of the best beaches, boardwalks, theme parks, water parks, scuba diving, light house tours, California wine tours, popular destinations, and much more.

Question 164: **I hate hotels. What are my other options for places to stay?**

Hotels are not always the most comfortable or economical means for traveling. In fact, many retirees are looking to stay longer at their featured destination and don't want to pay the expensive prices offered through hotels. There are many other options to help make your stay more enjoyable and easier on your wallet. For instance, house-swapping has become extremely popular. Intervac (*www.intervac.com*) is an organization that was started in 1953 by Swiss and Swedish teachers. They currently have over 11,000 homes in more than fifty countries around the world. The fee to join their organization online is only $79 for a year or $129 to receive their catalog.

Another option would be to join an organization called the Evergreen Club (*www.evergreenclub.com*). The club consists of more than 2,000 members who have signed up to play host during short visits by other travelers in the club. For as little as $15 a day per couple, you can stay for up to three nights in another member's guest room, and breakfast is included.

Question 165: **I'd like to travel with other seniors. What's the best way to find a group that coordinates these trips?**

Look no further than AARP's passport tours. The organization is focused on persons 50 and older and helps put trip packages together that meet the needs of seniors who are interested in traveling around the world. They offer substantial discounts through their last-minute packages as well. You can see all that the program has to offer by going to *www.aarp.org* and going to their travel link. Another great resource that caters to Americans over 50 is Grand Circle Travel. You can get a free catalog and more information by going to *www.gct.com*.

Question 166: **How can I travel for free or on a very tight budget?**

Credit cards offer some wonderful opportunities for you to earn free airline miles. Many offer programs in which you get a flier mile for every dollar you spend. Sometimes the cards will offer promotional deals for first-time users that include airline tickets, free companion passes, bonus miles, etc. You just have to check them out and see. Visit individual airlines' Web sites for further details.

To help minimize your costs for travel, read Lynie Arden's book *Travel Free: The Ultimate Guide to Bargain Travel*. It is packed with information on how to travel inexpensively or free.

Question 167: **What are some quick ways to get the latest travel promotions?**

One thing you can do is sign up for e-mail promotions through your favorite airline. You can join their frequent flier program and have them send you information on fare deals via e-mail. This is a great way to keep up with the specials without having to go out of your way to find them.

One great Web site to look at is Travelocity at *www.travelocity.com*. The site has information on flights, hotels, vacation packages, car rentals, and just about anything you'll need to plan your next vacation or business trip. Also check out *www.bestfares.com*, *www.budgettravel.com*, and *www.cheapertravel.com*.

Another quick promotional check would be through your local newspaper. Several major newspapers have a travel section that features travel destinations at special discount prices. Typically, they will have travel inserts in their Sunday papers that feature current deals and promotions.

Question 168: **What are some tips for travelers with disabilities?**

The Transportation Security Administration has helpful tips for travelers with disabilities, found on their Web site at *www.tsa.gov* (go to the For Travelers page). You can find answers to many questions such as what medications you can bring through the security checkpoints, procedures for medical equipment carry-on, and more. For additional consideration, AARP has outlined some key tips on their Web site found at *www.aarp.org*. They are:

- Provide advance notice to the airline you are flying if you will need additional assistance.
- Give the airline advance notice if you need a companion to accompany you through the checkpoint.
- Pack medications in a separate bag to help expedite the inspection process.
- Provide any necessary medical documentation to the inspector to help with the overall process.
- If you have diabetes, notify the screener that you are carrying necessary supplies to treat your condition.

- Certain medical devices, such as hearing aids, may be affected by the X-ray machine. You can reference the TSA Web site to confirm whether your device is able to pass through the X-ray machine safely.

Question 169: **What are some good online sites that rate resorts?**

Many useful sites and resources are available for you at no cost. If a destination sounds appealing to you and you think a hotel or resort looks charming, then consider checking out personalized reviews at *www.tripadvisor.com*. This site allows people to post their reviews on several hotels and resorts all over the world. They are honest and blunt. It also rates the location against other hotels and resorts in the area, which is helpful when your research gets overwhelming.

Question 170: **What are the benefits of using a travel agent?**

Planning for your next vacation can be an exciting yet overwhelming experience. By using a travel agent, you are utilizing the expertise and knowledge of a professional. Often the travel agent has been to the destination, or knows about the destination, that you are interested in. He can give you personalized advice that caters to your needs.

A good travel agent will let you know, in advance, when bargain fares are about to be announced. The other benefit to using an agent is that he has access to computer software that ensures you're getting the best airfare available, not just the best deal your agent could find at the time you booked your reservation. Agents can also be of great help in finding destinations that offer handicapped accessibility.

Question 171: **What is the best time to find airfare specials?**

The major airlines make more than 20,000 fare changes each day, so getting the cheapest fare requires careful planning. Look for airfare bargains right after major holidays. Believe it or not, the summer is a great time to find airfare deals. Business travel falls off during the summer and airlines are hustling to fill their planes. You can get the best airfare deals if you buy your tickets at least twenty-one days in advance. Wherever you go, always try to stay over on a Saturday, which can dramatically reduce your fare. If you are flying to attend a funeral, ask the airline about their bereavement policy, which could cut the fare considerably.

Question 172: **When is the best time to travel?**

Travel during the off-season. It's the best time to go anywhere and you can save 40 percent or more on your vacation. Often if you catch the front or tail end of the prime season, you get good rates, no crowds, and good weather. Typically, you will know when off-season starts because you get discounted rates. For example, Florida's peak season is the summer months. However, locals tell us that April and September are less crowded, have great weather, and feature cheaper hotel rates.

Question 173: **What is the best way to book a cruise?**

To get a fantastic cabin and a good rate, schedule your cruise way in advance through a travel agent who specializes in cruise travel. Cruising is a whole different ball game than other types of travel. Whether you are sailing to Alaska or the Caribbean, if you book your cruise as far as a year ahead, you'll save 30 percent or more. However, you can also get some great last-minute deals on cruises. The nice thing about cruises is that you typically get the food, lodging, and entertainment at one package price.

Question 174: **Should I consider joining a travel club?**

If you are really into traveling, then consider joining a travel club. Yes, you'll pay an annual fee, but because of their buying power, major travel clubs get access to tremendous travel packages that can exceed 50 percent off retail prices. When you join a club, you get a membership card, a directory showing where you can go at discounted rates, as well as newsletters that announce travel bargains. Major warehouse retailers such as Costco and Sam's Club offer travel discounts to their members.

Question 175: **I'm interested in adventure travel tours. What resources are available to help book these vacations?**

For one, REI is a great company that offers adventure travels, as well as retail gear for sale through their Web site, *www.rei.com*. For more than twenty years, they have been offering adventures in hiking, cycling, paddling, camping, and more. It may also behoove you to check with your local travel agencies. Many agencies are popping up around the nation, focusing on recreational and adventure travel.

Chapter 14

CONTINUING YOUR EDUCATION

Your pending retirement may open up the time you need to continue your education. The educational path can take a variety of twists and turns, depending on your specific interests and desires. For example, you may decide to take a class in digital photography so that you can explore all of the features of that new digital camera that you just got. Or you may decide to pursue that college degree that you have always wanted. A recent study by AARP discovered that 73 percent of the baby boomers polled expect to have a hobby or special interest take up most of their retirement. That means that of the baby boomers reaching retirement, 55 million are seeking hobbies or training for some sort of special interest. This chapter covers the many realms of continued education.

Question 176: What services are available for senior students going back to school?

The population of adult students is on the rise. You may be surprised to hear that the average age of community college students is 29, according to *www.colleges.com/admissions/articles/commtech.html*. Many schools have offered additional services to meet the needs of their aging student populations: financial aid, day care, work opportunities, support groups, and academic assistance, to name a few. In fact, many schools offer online and evening courses to cater to working adults and students with special needs. You will have to check with your institution of choice to determine its specific services.

Question 177: **How do I find the school that is right for me?**

There are many criteria you want to consider when determining the right school for you. For example, some things that might be on your list are the size of the classrooms, the structure and curriculum, and the school's accreditation. A very useful Web site that can help narrow your search for colleges is at *www.collegeboard.com*. They have a college matchmaker tool that will help you identify a school that is right for you based on your criteria. If you already have a school in mind, then you can use their college quick finder to get additional information on the college's profile. Both search options are found on the site's home page.

Question 178: **Are there any online education courses that are worth considering?**

Several mainstream universities offer virtual education through the Internet. Classes are videotaped and can, along with reading and assignments, be accessed online. Often you can take a class in the comfort of your own home at any hour of the day or night! Call or search the Web site of local universities or colleges to see if they offer online education courses.

In addition, universities have popped up everywhere that cater to the working adult who prefers a classroom with more mature adults sharing real-life experiences and pursuing a higher education.

If this level of education sounds appealing to you in your retirement, then consider the University of Phoenix, which is one of the more successful adult education programs in the nation. They offer online degree programs, as well as instructor-led programs. You can further research their program and curriculum at *www.uofphx.info*. There are also a variety of different colleges that offer many online programs. A good Web site to reference is *www.classesusa.com*.

Question 179: **I'm interested in attending a trade school. Can you help me find what I'm looking for?**

Perhaps you have come to realize that you have always put your dream job on the back burner. Possibly your interest in design, cookery, or art has intrigued you to look into a specialty school. There are a lot of different trade schools that cater to your every wish. You can begin your search by clicking on *www.collegesurfing .com*. This site allows you to search for your career of interest and finds colleges in the area where you live. Another helpful Web site is *www.trade-schools.net*. It's an informative Web site with several links to helpful references.

Question 180: **What are the different types of financial aid programs available for seniors/retirees?**

Continuing education has never been cheap, and finding the means to make it work can be a challenge. In fact, in their book *501 Ways for Adult Students to Pay for College*, Gen and Kelly Tanabe cover many new college programs set up for the aging population. For example, Oregon has the Senior Adult Learning Center program that does not yield credit hours, but does allow senior citizens to audit any Portland State University class as long as there is available space. If you want to find out specific information about the financial aid you may be eligible for, you can go to *www.finaid.org*. This site outlines the different types of aid and some of the factors you will need to consider when filing for aid. It can also answer questions about tax implications and what approach is right for you.

Another option is to call the U.S. Department of Education (800-433-3243) and ask them to send you an application for federal student aid. Study the application and become familiar with the questions you'll be required to answer so that you won't shortchange yourself. For example, a 401(k) plan or pension plan doesn't count as part of your current assets, so don't list them. As a general rule, approximately 6 percent of your assets and up to 50 percent of your income will be considered available for college expenses. Always keep those percentages in mind when you fill out the applications.

The entire process can be a bit overwhelming. To help walk you through it, consider getting a copy of *Complete Idiot's Guide to Financial Aid for College* by David Rye.

Question 181: **What are some tips that I should know before going back to school?**

It's important to have the tools necessary to get the most out of being an older student. We've outlined some tips to consider if you decide to go back to school:

- *Learn for less.* Many colleges offer senior programs with great incentives. You can check with the admissions office at your local college to determine which programs are offered.
- *Go online.* Many colleges offer online studies so you don't have to physically go to campus. If this is of interest to you, check the school's accreditation first at *www.chea.org* and then go to the Web sites of colleges you like to find out more about their online programs.
- *Get support.* Many colleges offer a wide range of assistance to help you get your feet on the ground and running. You can talk to the admissions office to get information on remedial classes, and to see if they have any senior support groups.

- *Study on the road.* Don't think it's too late to study abroad. Although you won't receive college credit, you can still participate in the program and take an Elderhostel trip. The prices vary based on the trip; you can get more information at *www.elderhostel.org*.

Question 182: **I love my hobbies. Where can I go to learn more about them?**

Retirement is a great time to review your hobby interests. If you're struggling with hobby ideas, two Web sites can help you. The first, *www.hobbylobby.com*, is a great Web site that offers all sorts of hobby interests and products. If gardening is of interest, then click on *www.hgtv.com*. You may also want to check out the different classes available through your local recreational center and any organizations that offer classes of interest. Another suggestion is to check out your local chamber of commerce Web site to see what classes they may be offering.

Chapter 15

USING YOUR PERSONAL COMPUTER

As more and more seniors go into retirement, the need to stay abreast and connected becomes extremely relevant in the fast-paced world of computers. Some retirees may be extremely comfortable with computers, and others might need some dusting off of their skills. This chapter helps you become more computer savvy. We've outlined frequently asked questions to help address your computer and Internet needs.

Question 183: **I would like to learn more about PCs. Do you have some ideas that will help me increase my knowledge?**

Several corporations offer online training for free or at a minimal cost. For example, if you want to learn the latest computer innovations, take IBM's online PC basics course geared to the entry-level computer owner. To access the training and get more information, go to *www.pc.ibm.com/training/mxw01.html.* Another company that offers specialized training is Dell. Their affordable PC training can be accessed online and they give you up to a year to complete your scheduled course. To view their selection and pricing, go to *www.dell.com* and type "online training" in the Search box.

If you prefer hands-on training, then consider looking into your local community college for PC courses. Whatever training method you choose, you can't go wrong with becoming familiar and comfortable with your personal computer. The technology is constantly changing, and it is always a benefit to stay ahead of the game. If you master your computer, you'll know how to make the most of its features and functions to meet your needs.

Question 184: **How can I learn more about World Wide Web technology?**

The Web is a magnificent tool that is literally at your fingertips. Our book references Web sites throughout because the Web is an extremely useful tool for gathering information. To feel more confident using the Web, it is best that you understand how the technology works. Several online resources can assist all levels of Web users. These resources can walk you through how the Internet works. One particular site, *www.learnthenet.com*, has easy-to-follow instructions for beginners. The site shows you how to connect your computer to the Internet, how to use the Web, and how to set up a Web site, and it offers useful tips and techniques to better understand and use the Internet.

For the intermediate Web user, learning about the latest technologies might be of interest. Wireless networking has taken the industry by storm. Consumers want to be able to access the Internet from anywhere. Therefore, you are starting to see phones and other handheld devices that offer the portability of the Web. Many coffee shops and restaurants offer wireless Internet to their customers for free.

Question 185: **How do I get Internet access in my home?**

Once you're familiar with the Web, start researching the different Internet providers that can connect your PC to the Internet and the Web. For a basic connection that will not cost you extra money, you can plug your desktop or laptop modem cord into your home phone line. There is no additional charge to your phone bill, and you can instantly access the Web. However, the fastest connection provided by the phone lines is 56K, and you can't use your network and your phone at the same time. When you are online, your phone will give a busy signal to incoming callers. If this setup is right for you, then you can instantly be online.

If speed is more your style, then you may want to consider DSL or cable modem. Several providers offer these services at a monthly rate. The monthly fee can be around $45 depending on the provider. A good site that provides all sorts of information on prices, options, and availability is *www.dslreports.com*. This will allow you to assess which configuration will work best for your online needs.

Question 186: **How can I go wireless?**

The Internet has made it easy for anyone to connect anywhere and everywhere. By going wireless, you can freely move around your home with your laptop and connect to your network, or you can use the many new devices to access the Web from anywhere. Several portable devices make this a breeze. At Microsoft's site (*www.microsoft.com*) you can search for all the latest and greatest technological advancements in wireless computing. You can go directly to *http://msdn.microsoft.com/msdnmag/issues/0600/Wireless* to answer many of your portable wireless connectivity questions. If you are more interested in setting up your home for wireless connectivity, then click on *www.microsoft.com/athome/moredone/wirelesssetup.mspx*. This article provides four steps and additional detailed information to get your home ready for wireless.

Question 187: **How do I set up a home e-mail account?**

Take advantage of e-mail; it's one of the greatest benefits of online technology. Most Internet service providers (ISPs) give their users free e-mail accounts with a certain amount of storage space for their mail. If you feel you need more storage space than the allotted free space, you can either purchase additional space or download your e-mail to your desktop to free up space on your account. Each provider will offer specific information about the terms of their e-mail accounts.

If you don't like the style of e-mail that your ISP offers, you can open a free account through some of the more popular Web portals such as Yahoo and Hotmail (*www.hotmail.com*). Either way, e-mail is a great tool to send mail quickly and at no additional cost.

Question 188: **What are some popular sites that I might need to know about now that I am retiring?**

Want to snag a $900 suit for $150? Try *www.ebay.com*. If you want to sell something of yours to your local community, post it on *www.craigslist.com*. If you're looking for a hard-to-find anthropology book, connect to *www.amazon.com*. You can even have your groceries delivered right to your door by *www.peapod.com*. Let's say you want to get technical product information and compare the specifications of several brands before you buy something. Try *www.compare.net* for a free online buyers' guide that allows you to compare thousands of products.

Question 189: **Can you provide me with a list of Web sites that I might find useful?**

Senior Travel Sites
www.elderhostel.com
www.tripspot.com/senior travelfeature.htm
www.aarp.org/travel

Selling of Goods
www.ebay.com
www.craigslist.com

Books
www.amazon.com
www.half.ebay.com
www.barnesandnoble.com

Cars
www.autobytel.com
www.carsmart.com
www.edmunds.com

Greeting Cards
www.bluemountainarts.com
www.evite.com
www.hallmark.com

Computer Hardware and Software
www.cnet.com
www.newegg.com
www.insight.com

Music
www.amazon.com
www.apple.com/itunes
www.columbiahouse.com
www.musicblvd.com

Senior Informational Sites
www.aarp.org
www.seniors-site.com
www.senior.com
www.senior-center.com

Chapter 16

TAKING CARE OF YOUR HEALTH AND WELL-BEING

Your retirement years can be one of the most enjoyable times of your life, if you manage to stay healthy. The risk of health failure increases dramatically with one's age—and a serious health issue can quickly bankrupt a lifetime of savings. The questions in this chapter have been designed to help you understand how to cover yourself financially should you incur a medical emergency.

Question 190: How do I know if my current health plan still works for me?

With the rising cost of health care, many insurers and employers are raising their health insurance premiums and cutting back on benefits. In fact, health insurance premiums have risen 70 percent in the past four years alone, according to *Money* magazine. Therefore, it's important that you review your current plan and make sure it still meets your needs. To determine if your plan still works for you, compare your plan with its competitors and see if the features from your plan match or exceed those offered in other plans. You may also want to consider getting any additional health plans such as John Hancock's extended insurance plans (*www.johnhancock.com*) so that you are fully prepared if you need to use it.

Question 191: **What health care plans do I need to consider?**

Read newspaper and magazine articles to stay abreast of what's going on in the Health Maintenance Organization (HMO) industry. HMOs represent one of the most affordable health programs you can get into today. HMOs sometimes run medical centers staffed with salaried doctors, nurses, and technicians, or they pay fees to a network of doctors and medical professionals who see patients in their offices. Point-Of-Service (POS) HMOs are a rapidly growing form of HMO that allows you to see doctors outside of the HMO group as long as you agree to pay the extra charges.

Preferred Provider Organizations (PPOs) are networks of doctors and hospitals that sign up with employers and organizations to treat patients at a discount. As with a POS, you can see doctors outside of the group if you pay the extra charges. Join an HMO, PPO, or POS and you will save money if you use the medical care that is within the organization that you join. Keep in mind that many of these organizations often limit their membership to specific groups, such as an employer or members of an association.

Question 192: **Which health insurance policy is right for me?**

First, consult a knowledgeable insurance agent and use her judgment to help narrow the field of providers. If you are insured through your employer, consider calling your human resources department to get additional policy information. Talk to your colleagues or friends and incorporate their judgments into your decision-making process, and subject potential medical plans to a financial test. How much are you willing to pay for monthly premiums and actual medical expenses? Consider out-of-pocket expenses, deductibles, and co-payment fees as well. Do a comparison chart of each policy against what you are looking for. This should help you decide which plan and policy meets your needs.

Question 193: **What can I do to keep my health care costs affordable?**

Find out if health insurance is available from any organizations to which you belong. Many religious, fraternal, and professional organizations provide health insurance for their members at competitive rates.

If you are on Medicare, select doctors who accept Medicare assignments. That is, they accept whatever Medicare pays and you are, therefore, not responsible for additional fees. You can find supporting doctors by going to *www.medicare.gov* and selecting search tools from their home page.

Always check your insurance plan before undergoing elective surgery. Call the insurer to make sure they cover all costs associated with the procedure before you commit to the surgery. Keep records of all phone calls and correspondence with your insurance company concerning the matter. It is highly advisable to get something in writing from your insurance company *before* you elect any procedures.

If you join an HMO, make sure you know their rules by heart and whom to call if there is ever a question. If you don't follow their rules, they may not pay your medical bills.

If you are paying a portion of the doctor or hospital bill, get an itemized statement that shows exactly what you're paying for. Hospitals are notorious for overcharging patients.

If there is a twenty-four-hour emergency clinic in your neighborhood, check out their prices. They're generally cheaper than hospital emergency rooms.

If you're overweight and smoke, lose weight and stop smoking. You are much more likely to get reasonable insurance premiums if you are in good health.

Question 194: **What steps can I take to reduce my prescription drug costs?**

With a few smart moves, you can cut your prescription drug bills by 50 percent or more. Here's how:

- *Go generic whenever you can.* If your doctor prescribes a brand-name drug, always ask if there is a generic equivalent. Generic drugs are usually known by their chemical names and are virtually identical to the better-known brand-name versions, but offer up to 70 percent in savings.
- *Look for substitutes.* If you're taking a brand-name drug for which no generic is available, ask your doctor or pharmacist if you can switch to a less expensive drug in the same category. In some cases, a substitute may even be available over the counter.
- *Comparison shop.* Prices for the same drug can vary dramatically between pharmacies. Start by checking prices at online pharmacies such as Costco.com, Familymeds.com or Drugstore.com. If you take a certain drug regularly, buying a ninety-day instead of a thirty-day supply can reduce your cost.
- *Find a good discount drug program.* For instance, Partnership for Prescription Assistance (*www.pparx.com*; 888-477-2669) provides a centralized data bank that makes it easy to learn about more than 250 public and private discount drug programs.

Question 195: **What is COBRA, and does it apply to me?**

If you leave your current employer, check into the availability of COBRA coverage. COBRA was an act passed by Congress (the Consolidated Omnibus Budget Reconciliation Act) that allows former employees of companies with twenty or more employees to keep their company health plan for eighteen to thirty-six months after leaving the company. Under the COBRA plan, a former employee retains the exact policy he had while working for his former employer. However, the employee must pay the premium to receive coverage. You are able to stay on COBRA for up to eighteen months for covered employees, as well as their spouses and dependents. If you are determined to have been disabled at any time during the first sixty days of COBRA, you have up to twenty-nine months of coverage. The maximum amount of coverage is up to thirty-six months for individuals who qualify based on the loss of employer-provided coverage due to an employee's death, divorce or legal separation, or certain "qualifying events." To find out more about COBRA, go to *www.cobrainsurance.net*.

Once your COBRA coverage is up, you have to look to an alternative insurance coverage policy. If you are having difficulty getting insured, consider the Blue Cross and Blue Shield Association. They are mandated by law to insure all people without regard to most of the criteria that commercial insurers normally use. That means you are assured coverage. However, it also means that Blue Cross often charges higher premiums because they can't refuse to cover people with prior medical problems or those who live in high-risk areas. You can read more at *www.bcbs.com*.

Many associations now offer medical insurance policies for their members. If your business is eligible for membership in an association, find out which ones offer health insurance coverage. Some states, including Hawaii, Vermont, Oregon, and Florida, are implementing their own universal health plans. Minnesota started Minnesota Care, a comprehensive program of state-subsidized health care. New York passed legislation that will force commercial insurers to take all applicants. New Jersey has also passed a subsidized insurance plan.

Question 196: **What are the different types of extended care facilities?**

The two primary types of care facilities are nursing homes and assisted care homes. Both are unique, so it is important to understand their differences.

A nursing home is a place where people live on a permanent basis because, for a variety of reasons, they are unable to take care of all their physical needs.

Assisted care homes, sometimes referred to as managed care homes, are a significant step away from nursing homes. People who live in managed care homes are capable of tending to all or most of their physical needs. In a typical care home, residents live in their own apartments and have the option of eating in a central dining facility. Well-run care homes offer a variety of activities for their residents to participate in, such as games, field trips, social gatherings, exercise classes, arts and crafts, and more.

Some things to be aware of with managed care homes are that they limit your medical choices in some ways. For example, although their facility has nursing staff that make themselves available twenty-four hours every day, you are expected to have your own network of doctors that will oversee your care. Should an emergency arise, managed care facilities have an emergency staff and equipped vehicles to transport you to an emergency or medical facility. Also, managed care facilities can cost less than half of what it costs to stay in a nursing home.

Question 197: **What are the chances that I will need long-term care?**

According to the National Association of Insurance Commissioners, one in every three persons aged 65 or older will spend some time in a nursing home. Not counting the patients who stay three months or less, one out of four will stay for four months to a year. About one out of ten will stay five years or more. The risk is much higher for women than it is for men. Medicare covers the first three months of your stay in a nursing home. After that time, you must pay the expenses associated with your care. Statistics show that needing long-term care at some point in your later years is probably inevitable. Thus, you should make it an important consideration for your retirement plan.

Question 198: **Should I get a long-term care insurance policy?**

It depends. You probably don't need long-term care insurance if you have assets in excess of a million dollars and can afford to pay for a nursing home yourself. If you would rather see your estate pass on to your spouse or kids when you die instead of using your own money to cover the cost of living in a nursing home, consider buying a long-term care policy.

When should you buy long-term care insurance? The younger you are, the cheaper it is. If you buy a policy at 50 and hold it for thirty-five years (to age 85), you will probably pay less for it than if you had bought the same policy at 75 and held it for ten years. Furthermore, you can't buy a policy unless you are in reasonably good health. So the longer you wait, the greater the risk that you won't be insurable.

Question 199: **How does disability insurance work?**

Disability insurance pays you a monthly income to help subsidize you during your inability to work due to an illness or accident. If the income that you are making before you retire is extremely important to your retirement plan, then you may want to obtain coverage that, when combined with other corporate or government benefits, will provide you with a minimally acceptable income.

Chapter 17

BUYING RECREATIONAL PROPERTY

As people retire, the thought of purchasing recreational properties, motor homes, and time-shares comes to mind and seems more appealing. In fact, in 2004, second-home sales went up 16.3 percent from the previous year, according to the National Association of Realtors. This chapter will help answer common questions to assist you in choosing a recreational property, investing in a time-share, or buying a motor home.

Question 200: **What's the best way to buy recreational property?**

Recreational property is generally thought of as real property that people enjoy because of its recreational features. It could be raw land that you use for camping or a swank condominium in Hawaii. In recent years, recreational property has become very popular with retirees who have dreamed about owning a place where they can "get away from it all."

If you're seriously thinking about this sort of investment, then consider how often you plan to use it. Assuming that you do not plan to use it full-time, will the property be safe from theft and vandalism when you're not there? Can it be insured? Can it be rented when you're not using it to provide you with an added source of income? Is it easy to get to and will the accommodations meet your needs as you age?

Question 201: **How can I determine if owning a vacation home is right for me?**

Owning a second home has become an alluring prospect for many retirees since the tax changes in 1997 took effect, which allows second-home owners to deduct interest payments and property taxes. In addition, many banks are now more willing to make loans on second homes. However, before rushing out to buy a second home, please review these considerations:

- **Pre-retirement home:** Before the capital gains tax rules changed in 1997, many people didn't purchase retirement homes until they sold their primary residence so they could roll over any gains from the sale of their current home into the new home. Today there is no need to wait, because the new law allows couples to roll over up to $500,000 of gain ($250,000 for singles) on their primary homes whenever they sell. If you're looking for a place that you can vacation in now and move to later, look at areas that have good health care facilities. If you plan to rent the property, does the area you are considering support a good job market and renter population? Look for states that have relatively low or no state income taxes, which can put money back into your pocket when you move.
- **Weekend getaways:** If you're thinking about buying a weekend getaway, make sure you buy one that you will really use on a regular basis. The last thing you want to happen is to buy a place that, for whatever reason, you don't

use. To help avoid this possibility, thoroughly check out any location you're considering and stay there for as many weekends as it takes to make sure it's the right area for you. If you plan to rent the property when you're not using it, check the tourism and hotel occupancy rates with the local chamber of commerce to get a feel for the short-term rental market.

- **Rental properties:** It is possible to find a second home that you visit once a year for vacation and rent out to tourists for the rest of the year at rental rates that cover your expenses. High-traffic tourist areas are ideal for this situation. However, bear in mind that IRS rules for this type of property can get complicated. If you use the house for fewer than fifteen days a year or less than 10 percent of the rental period, then it's considered a rental by the IRS. Your deductible expenses can't exceed your rental income.
- **Time-shares:** If you are only interested in staying at a vacation property you own for a couple of weeks each year, you may want to consider buying into a time-share rather than buying a second home. Time-shares may be appealing, but watch out for the high sales costs. For example, if you buy into a $10,000 time-share and decide to sell your share later, selling and marketing fees can easily be 40 percent or more of the sales price. A word of caution: The time-share resale market is almost nonexistent, so don't think of a time-share as an investment. Before you buy, verify the current tax laws on time-shares with your tax consultant and consider a consultation with a Realtor to discuss the resale value.

Question 202: **What exactly is a time-share property?**

When you purchase a time-share property, you technically own a "piece of time" in a particular complex or condominium. Essentially, you buy the right to vacation in the same or similar unit during a specified period of time every year (typically one to two weeks). For this privilege, you pay a purchase price and maintenance fees for your share of the ownership. Most desirable time-shares are located in great destinations.

Depending on the specifics of the investment deal you make, you can have limited to very flexible ownership in your share. With flexible time-shares, you can trade your time with other individuals and not be tied down to using your share at a particular time.

You can also purchase a fixed unit for a specified period of time each year that's written up in a deed agreement. Another option is a floating time-share arrangement where your time has more flexibility, but you are subject to reservations. This may provide a more feasible solution, but you may end up with scheduling conflicts, since it is based on a first-come, first-served scenario. A third option is a right-to-use agreement that mimics a lease. You have the rights to the unit until your lease expires. After that, you no longer have access to the unit.

The most flexible option is known as vacation clubs. This is a point-based system where you can choose from a variety of locations that are within the club you have purchased the time-share with. Each of your stays at a club location requires you to use points. These points fluctuate depending on the time of year, the quality of the unit, and/or the location. Major corporations, such as Starwood Hotels and Resorts, use point-based programs to capture interested customers. Typically, you will go through a separate time-share agency that assists with the negotiation of points and planning for your usage.

In simplest terms, time-share owners pay for their units. Then, depending on the unit you purchase, you may also have additional fees to cover maintenance, management, and upkeep costs associated with the complex that your unit is in. The extra fees should be disclosed at the time of purchase, and you should consider these when making a purchasing decision.

Question 203: **What are the advantages and disadvantages of owning a time-share?**

Advantages:

- Once you own it, the cost of staying in your time-share is usually cheaper than renting a comparable unit.
- You have the opportunity to meet and make friends with other time-sharers who stay in their units at the same time you do.
- Many time-shares allow you to swap your unit with someone else's at a different location.
- Owning a time-share can also yield tax breaks because it mimics the taxes associated with owning a second home.

Disadvantages:

- If you don't buy a good time-share in a desirable location, you may have a problem swapping it for another time-share or selling it in the future.
- If, for whatever reason, your lifestyle and/or desires change and you stop using your time-share, you will be paying for a vacation that you no longer take. Monthly principle payments and maintenance fees keep on accruing, whether you use it or not.
- Most people do not make money when they sell their time-shares. Sales fees can run 25 percent or more, so watch out.

Question 204: **What do I need to know if I decide to buy a time-share?**

If you decide to buy into a time-share, it is very important that you do your research. You want to be familiar with the laws associated with time-share property in the state where you are looking to purchase. You may also want to compare pricing and involve a Realtor to assist with this process.

Several resources are available to assist you with your research. For example, the Timeshare Users Group (*www.tug2.net*) offers a variety of topics online such as frequently asked questions, tips, advice, and much more. There are also several books available that can help you understand the basics of buying a time-share. Try *The New Vacation Revolution* by Alexander Barbara (and see his site at *www.vacationrevolution.com*) or *Timeshare Condominiums for the Beginner* by Michael Strauss to grasp the concepts and get your questions answered.

The better you understand time-sharing, the better negotiator you will be and the better deal you will be able to walk away with. There are several different alternatives you can opt for and it is necessary to thoroughly understand all of the options to make the best choice for your circumstances.

Question 205: **What should I be aware of when purchasing an RV?**

A recreational vehicle is the second most expensive purchase, after a home, that most Americans will make. There are several tips to prepare you for this big purchase so that you can avoid any pitfalls or mistakes along the way. You'll need to:

1. Understand the finance options for an RV.
2. Decide whether to buy a new or used RV.
3. Make the best purchasing choice for those on a budget.
4. Know whether to buy an RV or a trailer.

These and many more questions can be answered by one resource. The Better Business Bureau has put out a DVD, with the help of *www.rvtravel.com*, to help first-time buyers through the process. The DVD, *Buying a Recreation Vehicle*, offers straightforward and professional guidance to help consumers make the right decisions and usually save money without running into heartaches along the way. This DVD is available for $19.95 through *www.rvbookstore.com*.

Question 206: **What associated expenses go along with owning an RV?**

As you get more serious about buying an RV, you need to consider the insurance, payments, and possible financing for the model you prefer. The insurance for an RV will vary based on the anticipated usage, your past driving record, and other factors. To get an idea of the costs, you can go to *www.progressive.com*, *www.rv-insurance-coverage.com* or *www.rvinsurance.com*. Also, check with your current insurance provider to see if you can get a multiple-vehicle discount. To determine your financing options, ask whether there are any incentives through the RV dealer. You can also go to *www.rvusa.com* to see a list of financial groups.

Another expense is maintenance. You can plan for the maintenance expense by budgeting the expected yearly fees associated with the anticipated maintenance. You may also opt to purchase an extended warranty on your RV. You may decide to go with a minimalized RV that meets your needs and will not break your budget for repairs. For example, a newer pop-up trailer is going to require less maintenance than an RV that has 100,000 miles on it.

Finally, you will have general usage expenses. These include, but are not limited to, fuel, campground fees, food and supplies, and activity fees. To find out more about the overall expenses associated with RV living, go to *www.your-rv-lifestyle.com/rv-costs.html*.

Question 207: **What is the best way to budget for an RV?**

As gas prices go up, so does the cost of operating your RV. The best way to prepare for RV ownership is to budget for your personalized costs of usage. One thing that you may want to do when determining your usage budget is list the trips you plan to make and figure the gas cost based on the mileage of the trips. If you will need to store your RV, you will need to include the monthly fee for storage in your budget. Another factor to be calculated is the trip-planning details. If you are planning to stay in campgrounds, you will need to include the fees. If you plan to do certain activities at different destinations, you may want to calculate those costs into your budget. And don't forget, if you finance the RV, you will be making monthly payments. These are just a few of the costs to think about and include in your budget to make sure it aligns with your retirement plan.

PART IV

Putting It All Together

Chapter 18

CREATING AN ESTATE PLAN

Estate planning is not just for the wealthy. It is for anybody who wants to make sure their assets are handled properly and distributed to specific people (e.g., family members, friends, charities) in a predetermined way. If you do not create a formal transfer plan, your estate will be managed by the state and the courts—a lengthy and expensive process that more often than not leads to undesirable outcomes. We'll show you how to streamline the estate-planning process in the questions and answers that follow.

Question 208: **What is an estate plan?**

An estate plan arranges the distribution of assets in your estate when you die. And, if you become incapacitated, it can be used to make your wishes known in regards to your finances and personal care. Most estate planning begins with a will, which specifies who gets your property when you die. A living will is a supplemental document to a will. It allows you to spell out the medical treatment you want under specific circumstances. For example, you can specify whether you want life-support equipment under certain medical conditions so that your family members don't have to make the difficult decision on your behalf.

Question 209: **What key elements should I cover when planning my estate?**

Before you start drafting estate-planning documents, such as a will, you need to know what you want to accomplish with your plan. Naming the right people or institutions to carry out your wishes is essential to any estate plan. If you don't name someone, a judge will decide who will be responsible for administering the distribution of your estate after you die. If you need assistance in setting up your estate plan, contact a qualified estate-planning attorney. Ask your friends or colleagues for a referral. The National Network of Estate Planning Attorneys is available on the Internet at *www.nnepa.com*.

Question 210: **I would like to know more about estate planning. Where do I start?**

For starters, never underestimate what your estate is worth. Many people get caught up with the routine of just trying to make a living and struggling to pay the bills to the point where they grossly underestimate the size of their estates. As a result, they fail to take appropriate tax-saving steps. Taxable estates include home equity, retirement-account balances, life insurance proceeds, securities, and foreign assets. Make sure you know your true worth and assess it accordingly in your estate.

Another key task is to make sure you understand what you need to include in your estate plan—especially since this is probably the first time you have gone through this process. To help, pick up the book *Plan Your Estate* by Denis Clifford and Cora Jordan.

Question 211: How do I go about creating estate-planning documents?

When you create your will or trust, consider using an estate-planning attorney to help draft your will. You can draft one from do-it-yourself software, but any savings you may incur are hardly worth the risk of a mistake or oversight.

If you prefer to write the will or trust yourself, we caution you to do so only if your will is basic. Several software products can assist you with this process. The Learning Company offers a software product called Will Maker that is available at several computer stores and online at *www.nolo.com*. If you would like to read more about how a will works, pick up *Nolo's Simple Will Book* by Denis Clifford.

Question 212: Do I need a will?

Everybody needs a will, whether you are single or married, young or old, healthy or sick. By organizing your estate to your best advantage, you can ensure that your hard-earned money stays in the family or goes to the people and organizations of your choice. In most states, if you die without a will, your estate is passed through a prolonged and expensive process called probate. And if you fail to properly prepare for estate taxes, your estate could end up getting taxed at rates that may exceed 50 percent.

If you die without a will, the court takes over and, in effect, writes a will for you in accordance with the state's intestacy laws. You can rest assured that when the courts get done with your will, none of it will look like what you would have wanted. The court appoints an administrator for your estate and a guardian for your children if one is needed.

A will instructs your survivors about how to distribute your property; it also enables you to nominate a guardian to care for your children should they become orphaned. You designate someone whom you trust to act as your estate's executor (e.g., your spouse)—the person who will be responsible for taking inventory of your property, paying off your creditors and taxes, and ultimately splitting your estate among your heirs in accordance with the wishes you document in your will.

Question 213: **What things do I need to consider when I write my will?**

- **State laws:** Be careful that you do not bequeath property to heirs in a way that conflicts with state laws. Every state has laws that protect the interest of the spouse. In some states, a surviving spouse can claim as much as half of the estate, regardless of what you decree in your will.
- **Children:** You should specifically mention your children and close relatives by name in the will, even if you choose not to leave them anything. This covers you in case there is a question later that their omission was a result of an oversight or mistake.
- **Allocation:** Whenever possible, bequeath money in *percentages* rather than dollars. For example, if you own a mutual fund that is worth $100,000 today, its dollar value will fluctuate with market conditions. If your intent is to leave half of the fund to a niece, specify that your niece, by name, gets 50 percent of XYZ Fund.
- **Previous wills:** After you have drafted a will, destroy any previous wills and be sure you include the phrase, "I revoke all prior wills and declare this my last will and testament." File a copy of your will with your other important papers and make sure that key people know how to access it should something happen to you. Review your will when major changes occur in your life, such as divorce, marriage, birth of children, or relocation to another state.

Chapter 19

PREPARING YOUR TAXES

People probably experience more anxiety about taxes than they do about any other financial planning issue. However, as you move closer toward retirement, your taxes will, in all probability, be considerably less than they were during your working years. In this chapter, we will address questions and answers that will help you minimize the turmoil that is often associated with taxes.

Question 214: Should I consider using a professional to do my taxes when I retire?

A top-notch tax accountant can save you a lot of aggravation, and in many cases identify deductions that you have overlooked. The type of tax accountant you need will depend on the complexity of your return, where you are in your financial plan, and how much you're willing to pay. You basically have three options to consider:

- **Storefront tax preparers:** These are the people who work for companies such as H&R Block that maintain storefronts in mini-malls throughout the country. Most of these people are working part-time during the tax season and have been trained to ask you the right questions and fill out tax returns. They generally have a limited background in tax accounting, so do not expect them to offer you any strategic advice, which is a disadvantage of using storefront tax preparers.

- **Accountants:** Accountants, by our definition, are people who have a minimum of four-year college degrees in accounting. Most of them work as accountants for companies and moonlight out of their homes to earn extra money during the tax season. They have an edge over storefront tax preparers since they have accounting degrees and work full-time in the accounting field.
- **Certified Public Accountants (CPAs):** CPAs are considered the tax professionals of the industry. If you have a complex return, need tough questions answered on your current return, require year-round tax and investment-planning advice, and help just in case you're audited by the IRS, then you need a CPA. And yes, they are the most expensive route to go. However, a good CPA can become your most trusted financial friend and consultant throughout your life. If you don't mind paying the extra fees, it is the way to go. CPA firms are listed in the yellow pages, but you would be better off getting referrals from your friends and associates. Many CPAs operate independently out of home offices and charge rates that can be substantially lower than what full-blown CPA firms charge.

Question 215: **How can I get the most benefit out of a tax professional?**

Always arrive prepared when you meet with your tax professional. Most of them charge for their services on an hourly basis, so if you waste their time because you're not prepared, you'll pay for it. If you are meeting with one for tax and investment-planning advice, be prepared to tell him what you want to do in the current year and what your forecasted plans are for the next three to five years. Write your plans down in outline form so he won't have to take notes, which again takes time and costs you money.

Don't assume that your tax preparer is an expert in everything that's important to you. Do your own research and homework so that you can carry on an informed conversation about key topics. Also, keep him informed about any changes in your family situation that could affect your tax status, such as a divorce, a new baby, or a marriage. If you are considering taking a tax deduction that you think is legally borderline, give him all the facts and ask for his opinion about the risk of an audit. In other words, treat your tax professional as a strategic partner who is interested in helping you achieve your financial goals.

Question 216: **What can I do now to help reduce my taxes next year?**

After your return has been prepared by a tax-return professional, ask her what you can do to reduce your taxes next year. This may require a follow-up visit with your accountant after the tax season is over. Or, if you are using a seasonal accountant, ask for her advice at the same time you're having your return prepared. You may want to meet again with your tax preparer in November or December if you are considering dumping some stock and taking the loss, or, on the upside, selling and taking the capital gain hit. You may have some last-minute decisions to make on IRA or 401(k) investments to improve your overall tax situation.

Question 217: **How long do I need to keep my tax returns and records?**

According to the IRS, "you must keep your records as long as they may be needed for the administration of any provision of the Internal Revenue Code." Generally, this means you must keep records that support items on your return until the period of limitations for that return runs out. On their Web site, *www.irs.gov*, they explain the "period of limitations" by identifying the following considerations:

- In most cases, you are required to keep your tax return and backup records for three years.
- If you think the IRS may have questions regarding your income reporting, then keep records for six years.
- Keep all employment tax records for at least four years after the date that the tax becomes due or is paid, whichever is later.

Question 218: **What's happening to my property taxes?**

In the past five years, property taxes have risen 40 percent. Property taxes will keep rising nearly everywhere for homeowners even as house prices are falling in many parts of the country, according to a *USA Today* analysis of government data outlined in "Property Taxes Up As House Prices Fall" (April 24, 2007). Unfortunately, the quality of public education, which property taxes largely supports, has gone downhill in many sections of the country. In recent years, states such as Colorado and Oregon have been swept by anti–property tax groups that have managed to force tax levies back through the legislative process.

Question 219: **What can I do to lower my property taxes?**

You can do several things to lower your property taxes:

- *Find out if you qualify for any special property tax exemptions in your state.* For obvious reasons, most states don't publicize these. However, many states offer exemptions if you're older than 65, disabled, a veteran, or in other special group classifications.

- *Check the accuracy of your home's assessed value by reviewing the property record card that is on file at your assessor's office.* Most of the cards are now on a computer file. The card lists all of the features of your property upon which your tax is based, such as lot size, square footage, and improvements. If your home's features are overstated, you could be paying more taxes than you should, and you could refute the value to lower the taxes through the assessor's office.
- *If the value of your home is considerably higher than what other properties are appraised for in your neighborhood, and you can see no obvious reason for the increase, ask the assessor's office to provide you with an explanation.* If their explanation is not acceptable, you may have to hire a tax attorney to help you build a case for a lower appraisal. Watch out because that can be an expensive process to go through.
- *If you believe your home is assessed too high, document your case before you see the tax assessor.* If part of your case is based on the value of comparable properties in your neighborhood, you'll need written verification of three to five comparable homes. Photographs will help strengthen your case, so include those with your documents.
- *Make sure you follow the appeal process of your county's government to the letter.* Be unfailingly courteous whenever you talk to county officials. Anger won't cut it if you're trying to solicit their cooperation. If the county appeals board rejects your challenge, you can challenge the board in court at the state level or file your complaint with the state review board. That can be an expensive proposition and will probably require an attorney, so make sure it will be worth your time and money.

Chapter 20

PROTECTING YOURSELF WITH INSURANCE

The average American's wealth experiences a peak during the start of retirement. Therefore, properly covering your wealth and associated assets is important. It is also critical that you review your health and medical insurance closely at this stage in your life. You may be able to reduce some of your insurance plans and need to ramp up others. A single sickness or accident could cost everything you own and wipe out years of responsible financial planning. The following questions will help you prepare for the future, understand many aspects of insurance, and position yourself for full coverage through your retirement.

Question 220: **What do I need to know when I buy insurance?**

Most of us don't really know how much insurance we need. As a result, we tend to overinsure ourselves in insignificant areas and underinsure ourselves in significant areas. If you don't know what you are doing when you buy insurance, you will ultimately get hurt.

The pain comes when you have suddenly suffered a loss and find out, after the fact, that your insurance doesn't cover the catastrophe. It is important for you to assess the significant areas you need to insure. An excellent article to help walk you through what you may or may not need is at *http://articles.moneycentral.msn.com/Insurance/AssessYourNeeds/RetiringHeresTheInsuranceYouStillNeed.aspx*. Understanding what deductibles are reasonable for you to pay is an important factor that you should review. For assistance, go to *www.smartmoney.com*. The site offers worksheets to help you determine how much insurance you need.

Question 221: **What are insurance deductibles, and how can I use them to my advantage?**

An insurance deductible is what you will pay, out of pocket, before you collect the balance due to you by your insurance provider. For example, if you have a $100 deductible on your health care plan, then you will be responsible for paying the first $100 before your insurance will begin to pay for the rest of your care. You can use deductibles to your advantage because the higher the deductible, the less the insurance plan will cost you. Also, you can often deduct these from your taxes. This can give you some breathing room when it comes to health care costs. For example, if you get a minimal deductible, such as $100, then you will pay more each month than a plan with, say, a $1,000 deductible.

Question 222: **Should I buy all of my insurance from one company whenever possible?**

Often you can experience a discount in the cost of insurance when you buy all of your insurance from one company. Purchasing your home, car, and health insurance from one provider can save you hundreds of dollars. It is worth getting several quotes from reputable companies and inquiring about combining all of your insurance under their umbrellas. Once you have their quotes, then compare the quotes and deductibles to find the best rates.

Question 223: **What does homeowner's insurance cover?**

Most homes are insured with a homeowner's policy that combines property insurance and personal liability insurance. Your property insurance covers your home, its furnishings, and your personal belongings. If your home was destroyed by a fire, for example, you would have to spend a considerable amount of money to replace your furnishings. Personal liability insurance covers individuals or members of a household against claims from third parties. Mortgage lenders require homeowner's insurance on a house before they will approve a loan.

Question 224: **What's the best way to save money on my homeowner's policy?**

One of the biggest opportunities you have to save money on your homeowner's policy, without taking on significant risk, is in the personal property part of your policy. Homeowner's policies do carry a deductible. The deductible could range anywhere from $0 to $1,000, or more. Here's how personal property liability and associated deductibles work. Generally speaking, personal property in and around your home is covered from perils such as fire and theft by your homeowner's policy. Most good homeowner's policies also cover your personal property when you're away from home, such as a camera that's stolen out of your car.

Make sure you shop different insurance companies for the best homeowner's rates. Prices can easily vary by 25 percent or more, depending on the company. For example, if one company is experiencing unusually high claim rates, they will simply increase their rates to all their holders.

Question 225: **What are some money-saving tips I can use when buying insurance?**

- Install deadbolts, smoke detectors, a fire extinguisher, a burglar alarm (even a cheap one), and you'll get a discount on your insurance. You should do all these things even if you don't get an insurance discount.
- Pay your premiums annually rather that accepting your provider's payment plan and high billing fees.
- Quit smoking and take the nonsmokers discount.
- If you have a second home, insure both homes under the same company and get the multiple home discounts.
- Insurance companies are regulated by state governments. Call your state's insurance office and ask them to send you a rate comparison.
- Don't over- or underinsure. For example, if your house is worth $100,000 and you insure it for $200,000 and it gets destroyed by fire, the most you'll get is $100,000. By the same token, don't underinsure your home. If your house is worth $100,000 and you insure it for $50,000, you'll only get $50,000 if it is destroyed.

Question 226: **How do I know if I'm adequately covered on my homeowner's policy?**

Most policies state that your home must be insured for a minimum percentage of its replacement cost, which excludes the land and foundation. If your policy contains this clause followed by a percent that is less than 100 percent (e.g., 80 or 90 percent) you might want to increase your coverage to 100 percent. For example, if your house is worth $100,000 (excluding the land and foundation) and your current policy only covers 80 percent, that means you would have to cover the remaining $20,000 ($100,000 minus 80 percent) yourself if your home was destroyed. Usually, the cost to increase your coverage to 100 percent is relatively low, and you'll have peace of mind knowing that your home is completely covered.

Question 227: **What does auto insurance cover?**

It is important to understand the major areas covered by auto insurance and determine how much insurance you will need in each of the following categories:

- **Bodily injury liability:** Liability coverage protects you financially if your car injures or kills someone. Because you could be liable for a large sum, you should obtain as much of this coverage as you can afford.
- **Property damage liability:** If you are at fault in an accident, property damage coverage not only pays for the damage that your car causes to another person's car, but it also covers any damage your car might do to other property, such as a trailer or a building.
- **Medical payments:** This coverage pays for medical bills from injuries suffered in an accident. It's a relatively expensive form of medical insurance and may not be necessary if you already have medical insurance. Auto medical insurance pays to the limits of the bodily injury portion of the policy for anybody injured in your car regardless of who was at fault.
- **Collision:** This coverage pays for damage to your vehicle, no matter who or what caused it. Premiums vary with the value of a vehicle and the amount of the deductible. If you are driving an older car, it probably doesn't pay to buy collision coverage. The repair bill for anything other than minor damage may exceed the cash value of your car. If that is the case, the insurer considers the car "totaled" and pays you the value of the car.
- **Comprehensive coverage:** Comprehensive picks up where collision leaves off. It insures your vehicle against theft, damage from falling objects, earthquakes, floods, or collisions with animals. You can choose to just have comprehensive coverage if you opt out of collision coverage.
- **Uninsured and underinsured motorist coverage:** This covers you if you're involved in an accident with an

uninsured or underinsured driver, or if you are a victim of a hit-and-run driver.

Question 228: **What are my options for life insurance, and how do they compare?**

The two types of insurance to consider are term versus whole life insurance. Term life insurance is payable to a beneficiary when the insured person dies within a specified period of time. If the insured individual is living at the end of the period, then the policy expires without value and nothing is paid out to that individual. Whole life insurance is payable to the beneficiary at the time of death of the policyholder, at whatever point that occurs. It also offers premiums payable for a specified number of years (defined as limited-payment life insurance) or for life (known as straight life insurance). Now that you know the different types of insurance, you can begin to get more information and understand which policy will work best for you.

All insurance companies would prefer to sell you a whole life policy, or a derivative thereof, rather than a cheap term policy because there is more money for them in the former. Life policies typically build up a cash value over time. As you would expect, they cost a lot more money than a term policy. Again, compare their cost and added features to what you would pay for a term policy so that you can make an intelligent decision as to what's best for you.

One way to start your comparison shopping is to contact Insurance Information Inc. (800-472-5800). If you're interested in term insurance, they will send you insurance quotes from more than 500 companies that have the lowest quotes for someone with your insurance profile (age, sex, smoker, nonsmoker, etc.). They charge a fee for this service. Also, contact Wholesale Insurance Network (888-898-2962) for low-cost term and whole life policy quotes over the phone. You can also reference the article found at *http://money.cnn.com/2002/12/17/pf/expert/ask_expert*.

Question 229: **Should I buy a term life insurance policy?**

Like auto insurance or homeowner's insurance, term insurance buys you pure protection. Its sole function is to provide financial support to your family or people you care about if you die. As is the case with any life insurance, the price increases as you get older. If you try to buy term insurance when you are in your sixties, you probably won't want to pay the "expensive" premiums. That's okay as long as you have built up sufficient savings to cover your spouse if something should happen to you and if all of your dependents are grown.

On the surface, term insurance would seem to be much more preferable than whole life since it is considerably cheaper. However, whole life insurance policies come packaged with savings accounts. Term policies end in a specified number of years, such as ten or twenty years. If you still need insurance coverage when your term policy runs out, you can always renew it if you're in good health. If you develop bad health conditions such as high blood pressure, you may be uninsurable, which is a major disadvantage of term insurance.

Question 230: **What is the primary advantage of whole life insurance?**

Whole life insurance remains in effect for the rest of your life, regardless of your physical condition. Whole life insurance, which is sometimes called cash value insurance or permanent life insurance, is expensive, but it offers several benefits over term life that are worth considering. For example, whole life insurance offers death benefits. This means that you get at least some of, and often much more than, the amount you spent on your premium. Another benefit is that the premiums typically stay the same throughout the terms of the policy. Finally, if you are a conservative investor and have difficulty saving, traditional whole life insurance makes sense because it acts as a "savings account." These policies come packaged with all kinds of different features that are unique to each company offering them.

Question 231: **Should I consider buying a whole life insurance policy?**

Whole life covers you with life insurance for your entire life. At some point, you will die and your whole life benefit will pay off. As we mentioned earlier, these policies accumulate a cash value over time. It usually takes at least five years before you will begin to build up cash value in your account. If you keep the policy long enough, your annual cash value can exceed the premium payment because of compound interest.

Insurance agents will be quick to tell you that over time, the life insurance part of your whole life policy costs you nothing because the cash in your account is generating enough interest to pay the annual premium. That's not true because the earned interest is *your* money that's paying the premium. Premiums for whole life typically remain the same over the life of the policy unless you pick one that has graduated premium rates.

Question 232: **In a nutshell, what's the advantage of term insurance over whole life insurance?**

Term insurance is great if you need a lot of cheap life insurance coverage over a specified number of years and you can simultaneously replace the protection it provides by building your investment portfolio. For example, if you have a health problem, you may want to carry additional life insurance now to cover your spouse while you settle your retirement. Whole life insurance policies are great if you want to have life insurance protection when you are in your seventies or eighties and need something that will force you to save money each month through monthly insurance payments. As mentioned previously, most whole life policies build up a cash value over time.

Question 233: **How much life insurance do I need?**

Like your retirement plan, an insurance plan should cover your financial needs in the event that your death adversely affects your loved ones financially. If you're married and living off two incomes, you and your spouse need to address the financial ramifications of one of you dying prematurely. Could the surviving spouse sustain your joint financial commitments (such as a mortgage, car payments, debt and loan payments) on a single income?

How do you determine how much life insurance you really need? One approach would be to multiply your combined incomes by the number of years your children will be dependents in order to get an estimate. For example, let's assume that you and your spouse have a combined annual income of $75,000. You have two children, ages 15 and 17, who you have decided will remain dependents until they reach the age of 21. The amount of life insurance coverage could be calculated as follows:

Coverage = Combined Incomes × Dependent Years Remaining/Number of Dependents

So using our example from above:

Coverage = $75,000 × (6 + 4)/2

Coverage = $375,000

Each spouse would need to purchase a life insurance policy equal to one half of the total amount needed (in this example, $375,000/2 or $187,500) to be able to cover the lost income if one of them were to die. In our example, we arbitrarily assumed that each spouse earns the same amount of money, or $37,500 after taxes a year, to simplify our illustration. If one spouse is earning more than the other spouse, the insurance coverage on the higher wage earner would be prorated. In either event, the calculated amount of insurance would be sufficient to cover the lost income should either spouse die before the kids become independent at age 21.

Question 234: **If I decide to buy life insurance, how can I find a good, inexpensive policy?**

We've listed several ideas to help minimize your life insurance costs, while keeping the quality of your plan strong.

- **Always keep it simple.** In its simplest form, you buy a life insurance policy that will pay your designated beneficiaries a specific amount of money if you die. Listen to the options your agent pitches to you, but don't lose focus on what you truly need.
- **Shop around.** When you shop for life insurance, contact at least two companies that you can negotiate with at the same time. All of them have different life products to offer at widely varying fees.
- **Establish a baseline.** In the interest of keeping it simple, get a price for a plain-vanilla term life policy in the amount that you need. It is the cheapest form of life insurance offered. You buy a specified amount of coverage (e.g., $100,000) for a term of years (e.g., 5 years). At the end of the term, the policy expires. It's as simple as that.

Chapter 21

FINALIZING YOUR RETIREMENT PLAN

Retirement planning is the process you go though to develop a financial plan that will cover you during your retirement years. We've addressed well over a hundred retirement planning issues in the previous chapters. It's now time to consolidate everything you've learned into a simple retirement plan.

Question 235: What's changed in retirement planning?

In the old days, retirement planning was simple. Once you turned 65, you collected social security and an employer pension, moved to Florida, and lived happily ever after. Well, not anymore! With time, that has all changed. Many people want to retire early; many others want to work longer. Guaranteed pensions are disappearing and are being replaced with self-directed retirement plans. As a result, retirement planning has become more complex and more important.

Question 236: **Why is my retirement plan so critical?**

At a time when employers are dropping guaranteed pensions and social security is struggling to meet the increased financial demands of the retiring baby boomers, what's a person to do? Take a proactive approach and develop the best retirement plan you can that meets your exact expectations and any potential future problems.

A well-coordinated retirement plan will help you get through a time of your life when, financially, you are probably going to be living on less than you're used to. Retirement planning incorporates a multitude of subplans to assure that your happiness and financial well-being are maintained during your retirement years. People who choose not to take the time to develop a retirement plan usually end up not knowing where they've been, and they have no idea where they're going.

Question 237: **What should my basic plan include?**

Your plan should include a wide variety of things. To find out the contents of a plan, consider reviewing an existing tool that is created to help you with your planning process. For example, Fidelity Investments offers several excellent retirement planning tools on their Web site (*www.fidelity.com*). Click on the "Retirement and Guidance" option that appears in the upper center section of Fidelity's main menu to get started.

Question 238: **What documents should I include in my retirement plan?**

All legal documents and any material that is pertinent to your plan should be included in your retirement plan folder. Having a completed plan with all relevant information and paperwork just makes it less complicated and easier to get at. On the following pages, we've listed the three key components that should be in your plan:

1. Savings plan: A monthly plan that shows what you have currently saved and what you plan to save throughout your retirement years. It helps to show where you are financially and where you are planning to be throughout your retirement years.
2. Insurance policies: Including these documents makes it much easier on whoever has to follow up on this information in the future. For example, if you are a widow and you supply your retirement plan to your only daughter, you have a vested interest in making sure she has all the information she may need one day. If you were to become seriously ill, she would most likely need to step in and assist by following up on your insurance policies. Therefore, keeping her or anyone else you choose current on your insurance status is critical.
3. Investment portfolio: This goes along with what was said about your insurance policies. Keep your plan as financially current as you can. Situations can change and you want to make sure that your trusted person (possibly the holder of your power of attorney if something were to happen to you) has all of your investment information so that she can engage as needed.

Question 239: **What resources are available online to help me create my retirement plan?**

There are several good resources to help you create your retirement plan online. Most financial institutions offer sections on their Web sites to assist with planning for your future in retirement. Here are a couple of great resources to help get you started:

- *www.fidelity.com*
- *www.ssa.gov/retire2*
- *www.401k-site.com*
- *www.aarp.org*

Question 240: **Where can I find legal will forms?**

There are several software programs you can purchase that walk you through the process of making a will. They offer the legal forms that you can use when you finalize your will. One software application that is extremely popular is WillMaker. You can purchase it online through any software retailer such as *www.amazon.com*, at a local office supply store such as OfficeMax, or at *www.nolo.com*. You can also find resources for will documentation online. Some sites that provide this are *www.findlegalforms.com*, *www.legaldocs.com*, and *www.uslegalforms.com*.

Question 241: **Do I need to use a notary for my finalized will?**

To be valid, a will must be legally executed. This simply means that you must sign your will in front of witnesses, not necessarily a notary public. The designated witnesses must sign the will in front of you, as well as in the presence of the other witnesses. Most states require two witnesses per will. You will want to check your state requirements if you are going to have witnesses. Some individuals may choose to have a notary public sign an affidavit under oath, so that each witness would not have to appear in court if the will and/or its content is in question.

Question 242: **What are the primary types of professionals that can help me prepare my retirement plan?**

- See a *certified financial planner* to obtain an objective opinion and overview of your retirement plan.
- See a *certified public accountant (CPA)* for tax planning, budget planning, personal business advice, and retirement income projections.
- See an *insurance agent* for a review of the insurance policies that you may or may not need to supplement your retirement plan.

- See a *securities broker* to set up an IRA or a 401(k) plan or to buy securities on your behalf to augment your retirement plan.
- See a *trust attorney* to set up a will or living trust to protect your loved ones in your plan.

Question 243: **Exactly what is a financial planner?**

Generally speaking, a financial planner is a person who makes a living assisting people in developing and implementing financial plans that are customized for them. A good financial planner works with you on an ongoing basis to help build your portfolio. Certified financial planners must take a five-part course, pass a ten-hour exam, and complete fifteen hours of additional training a year to become certified.

Question 244: **What expert qualifications do financial planners have?**

Many financial planners have security licenses, allowing them to sell you the financial products they may recommend to you. They can also be CPAs who specialize in personal finances with the added benefit that their accounting experience gives them tax expertise. Many stockbrokers have moved into the financial planning area to attract more clients. Clearly, financial planners can take on many professional forms. If you feel you need one, the professional form is as important as the level of confidence you establish with whomever you're working with.

Question 245: **Should I hire a professional to review my retirement plan?**

You may not need the services of a professional financial planner on an ongoing basis. A periodic consultation with your broker or accountant may be sufficient to manage your portfolio, since basic financial planning isn't hard to do. To be your own planner, you'll need a list of objectives for any financial products that you own, and for financial products that you're tracking for possible future investments. Under certain circumstances, you may need to work with a financial planner on a regular basis:

- You earn a good wage, but cannot manage to save anything on a regular basis.
- You're facing a tough investment question that you feel can't be answered without some expert advice.
- You've got a savings and retirement plan in place that is just sitting there making money without any help from you.

Question 246: **If I decide to hire a financial planner, what qualifying questions should I ask him?**

One of the first rules about selecting a financial planner is that you must spend an adequate amount of time looking for and assessing their qualifications. Keep your eyes peeled for telltale warning signs that may come up when interviewing planners. One of the most suspicious is a refusal to let you talk with their clients for a reference. Here are important questions to ask:

- What are their qualifications, including special designations and training?
- What's their investment style?
- What sort of clients does the planner work with and do any have financial situations similar to yours?
- Will the planner you're interviewing service your account or will it be handed off to a subordinate?

Question 247: **What does it cost for expert advice?**

Fidelity Investments offers a service that's free even if you are not a Fidelity client. It's called the Fidelity Retirement Income

Advantage and it is designed for people within ten years of retirement. One of their financial planners will create a comprehensive retirement income plan, including a withdrawal strategy, to help you meet expenses. Charles Schwab also offers free support; you can get more information at *www.schwab.com*. Check with your main financial resources or favorite financial institution to see what expert advice they offer to their clients.

Question 248: **Who needs a copy of my retirement plan and why?**

It is always a good idea to give backup copies of your retirement plan to trusted individuals. This may include people who are written into your plan, such as your children or siblings. To answer this question correctly, just think about who would need to have a copy of your plan in case something happened to you. Then make sure that those individuals have copies or know where to find a copy as needed.

Question 249: **What are some tips you can provide as I begin to plan for retirement?**

All of us would like to be financially independent. To get there, many people try any get-rich-quick scheme that comes along, including the lottery. They'll invest in whatever somebody tells them is a ground-floor opportunity to make it happen. Others will adopt a more scientific approach and, with all good intentions, seek out the advice of an investment broker and invest in something without much thought.

Even though we may try completely different investment approaches, most of us share two common failings: our financial plans are not consistent, and if we managed to set goals, we will not follow them to achieve the financial security we want. As a result, many people will move into their retirement years subsisting on substandard retirement incomes. We caution you to be realistic when you create your retirement plan and follow the guidelines we have given you to achieve the financial independence you seek in order to retire.

Question 250: **What final thoughts can you share with me regarding my financial future?**

If you start with a financial plan, a solid set of financial goals, and work out from there, you will become financially independent. If you already have a retirement plan in place, great! If you don't, then start one today. If you are fortunate enough to own a home, a retirement plan combined with a home that's paid off are two of the most important steps you can take to secure your financial future. The rest is up to you.

APPENDIX OF WEB SITES BY SUBJECT

Analyst Evaluations

Finding out what stock analysts are saying about a stock that you're considering can help you determine if it's the right time to buy. Here are several sites that will get you the information you need:

VectorVest (*www.vectorvest.com*) offers free reports showing what your stocks are really worth, how safe they are, and when to buy, sell, or hold. It's one of the best analyst's sites on the Internet.

S&P Advisor Insight (*www.advisorinsight.com*) allows you to review Standard & Poor's reports for major stocks.

Zacks Investment Research (*www.zacks.com*) reports on what analysts are saying about most of the stocks on the U.S. exchanges.

Annual Reports of Publicly Traded Companies

Investor Guide (*www.investorguide.com/stocklist.cgi*) provides links to thousands of publicly traded companies.

Best Calls (*www.bestcalls.com*) provides access to companies' quarterly earnings press conferences.

Investor Relations Information Network (*www.irin.com*) offers hundreds of company's annual reports online.

Public Register's Annual Report Service (*www.prars.com*) offers both online and hard copy annual reports.

Thomson Investor Net (*www.thomsoninvest.net*) covers more than 7,000 in-depth company reports that are updated twice a month.

Security Exchange Commission (SEC) is the official government site that hosts all financial reports of the publicly traded companies in the United States. The site is at *www.sec.gov /edgar/searchedgar/webusers.htm*

Associations

American Association of Individual Investors (*www.aaii.com*) offers a variety of valuable services to their members, including local chapter meetings in the major metropolitan areas.

The National Association of Investors Corporation (NAIC) is a national association with local chapters throughout the country. Their goal is to help investors develop a disciplined approach to successful investing. For more information, visit their Web site at *www.better-investing.org*.

Bonds

Bonds Online (*www.bondsonline.com*) provides charts and historical data that compare the various bond market sectors.

The Bond Market (*www.bondcan.com*) specializes in investing in Canadian bonds.

The Bond Market Association (*www.bondmarket.com*) is loaded with information about thousands of bonds and their respective trading history.

Brokers (Online)

Accutrade (*www.accutrade.com*) 800-494-8939

American Express (*www.americanexpress.com*) 800-658-4677

Morgan Stanley (*www.morganstanley.com*) 212-761-4000

E*Trade (*www.etrade.com*) 800-387-2331

Fidelity (*www.fidelity.com*) 800-544-8666

Muriel Siebert (*www.msiebert.com*) 800-872-0444

Schwab (*www.schwab.com*) 800-435-4000

Wall Street Access (*www.wsaccess.com*) 800-925-5782

TD Ameritrade (*www.tdameritrade.com*) 800-669-3900

Diversified Planning

Legg Mason's Web site (*www.leggmason.com*) provides an online questionnaire to help you develop a diversification plan.

Frank Russell Company (*www.russell.com*) features a Comfort Quiz to help you allocate your investments.

Fidelity's Asset Diversification Planner (*www.fidelity.com*) offers diversification advice, a risk questionnaire, and five model portfolios.

The Intelligent Asset Allocator (*www.efficientfrontier.com*) offers comprehensive information on how to build a diversified portfolio.

Economic Information and Trends

The Bureau of Economic Analysis (*www.bea.gov*) calculates economic indicators such as the gross domestic product and other regional, national, and international data, all of which are displayed on their Web site.

Census Bureau (*www.census.gov*) provides information about industry statistics and general business conditions.

STAT-USA (*www.stat-usa.gov*) is sponsored by the U.S. Department of Commerce and provides financial information about economic indicators, statistics, and economic news.

Education

The American Association of Individual Investors offers advice on funds and portfolio management on their Web site at *www.aaii.com.*

Bloomberg Personal Finance (*www.bloomberg.com*) offers online training when you click on the Bloomberg University module.

SEC information for seniors (*www.sec.gov/investor/seniors.shtml*) Investing Wisely offers a series of educational articles for senior investors.

Investing Basics (*www.aaii.com/invbas*) offers feature articles about how to start successful investment programs, pick winning stocks, and evaluate your options.

Investor Guide (*www.investorguide.com*) features more than 1,000 answers to frequently asked questions.

Money 101 provides a crash-course, interactive investment seminar at *www.money.cnn.com.*

Money and Investing (*www.eldernet.com/money.htm*) offers tutorials and advice on investing in stocks, mutual funds, and bonds.

Morningstar's University (*www.morningstar.com*) offers a comprehensive investment education program.

The Motley Fools offer an investment seminar on their Web site at *www.fool.com.*

The Mutual Fund Education Alliance is the trade association for no-load funds and offers advice on how to select funds (*www.mfea.com*).

Vanguard (*www.vanguard.com*) offers online courses that cover the fundamentals of investing in mutual funds.

Exchanges (Stock)

The American, NASDAQ, and New York Stock Exchanges offer a wide variety of investment features that may appeal to you.

American Stock Exchange (*www.amex.com*).

The National Association of Securities Dealers (*www.nasdaq.com*).

The New York Stock Exchange (*www.nyse.com*).

Financial Tools and Calculators

The Web sites that we have listed in this section offer a multitude of solution-oriented features.

The Financial Center (*www.financialcenter.com*) has a section for retirees. Choose United States and then financial planning. Under this category, choose retirement.

Schwab (*www.schwab.com*) helps you develop a financial plan with its online calculators, tools, and advice.

Games (Stock Market)

Virtual Stock Exchange by Market Watch (*www.virtualstockexchange.com*) is a stock-simulation game that allows you to trade shares just as you would in a real brokerage account.

Indexed Funds

There are literally hundreds of mutual funds that index every segment of the market. Here are two of the better funds to consider:

Fidelity Spartan Market Index Fund, which mirrors the Standard & Poor's 500 (S&P 500) index (800-544-8888)

T. Rowe Price Equity Index Fund, which mirrors the S&P 500 (800-638-5660)

Industry Information

ABC News (*www.abcnews.com*) features articles on current industry news and market expert commentary.

American Society of Association Executives (*www.asaenet.org*) provides high-quality industry overviews including briefings of industry trends.

Hoovers Online (*www.stockscreener.com*) offer excellent information on industries at their Web site.

Research magazine (*www.researchmag.com*) offers helpful references to industry news, columns, and highlights.

International Investing

The Internet is rich in sources for information on foreign companies. Three Web sites in particular with useful information are *www.bankofny.com*, *www.jpmorgan.com*, and *www.global-investor.com*. Also, FT Market Watch (*www.ftmarketwatch.com*) provides up-to-the minute news on offshore companies and foreign markets.

Investment Strategies

Bank of America's Web site (*www.bankamerica.com*) offers a retirement center under the heading Achieve Your Goals on their main menu. It has several useful references for advice for retirees.

Investor Home (*www.investorhome.com*) provides information about the investment process and how to bulletproof your portfolio.

Magazines

Business Week (*www.businessweek.com*) is available online to all of its subscribers.

Forbes (*www.forbes.com*) is available online and features articles on personal finance and investing.

Fortune (*www.fortune.com*) includes special market reports as well as stock and fund quotes.

Kiplinger's (*www.kiplinger.com*) has a broader scope than either *SmartMoney* or *Worth*. Instead of talking just about investing, *Kiplinger's* moves into other issues of personal business, such as credit card spending, loans, college tuition, and vacation planning. For subscription information, call 800-624-2946.

Newsweek (*www.newsweek.com*) not only covers the general news but also covers the latest news about the stock market.

SmartMoney is the "*Wall Street Journal* magazine of personal business" and it's excellent. For subscription information, call 800-444-4204 or visit their Web site at *www.smartmoney.com*.

Worth columnists, including Peter Lynch, are second to none, and the magazine's regular features are dynamite. For subscription information, call 800-777-1851 or go to *www.worth.com*.

Money does an excellent job of keeping its readers informed about what's happening in the mutual fund market. For subscription information, visit their Web site at *www.money.com*.

Mutual Funds: General Information

There are almost as many mutual funds to choose from as there are stocks. The following Web sites will help you find the best ones out there:

CBS Market Watch (*www.marketwatch.com*) provides articles, news, and market data on funds.

MaxFunds (*www.maxfunds.com*) specializes in offering news and statistics on small and little-known funds.

Morningstar (*www.morningstar.com*) is a premier site providing all kinds of information about mutual funds.

Mutual Funds: Ordering Online

Fidelity (*www.fidelity.com*) offers direct purchase plans for its funds.

Janus (*www.janus.com*) has a family of no-load funds that you can purchase or apply for online.

Money magazine (*www.money.cnn.com*) offers a wealth of knowledge in all aspects of money and finances.

T. Rowe Price (*www.troweprice.com*) offers direct purchase plans for its funds.

Vanguard (*www.vanguard.com*) has more than eighty funds that you can purchase directly from the company.

News Online

One of the biggest advantages of getting your news online is that you can go to the specific news sector (e.g., Market Watch) without having to thumb through a bunch of paper to get there. Here are several excellent sites to try:

ABC News (*www.abcnews.com*) features business and industry news and market commentary.

Bloomberg Personal Finance (*www.bloomberg.com*) is loaded with timely business news, data, and an analysis of the market.

News Page (*www.newspage.com*) allows you to customize daily news abstracts that it sends to your e-mail address.

Newspapers

Financial newspapers are still a way of life in the stock market's paper-oriented world, although some of them are beginning to make the migration over to the online sector. Here's a rundown of the best papers that are out there:

The *Financial Times* (*www.ft.com*) provides special reports on the market and the different industry sectors.

Investor's Business Daily is a great financial newspaper that publishes important information to help determine the value of a stock. For subscription information, call 800-831-2525 or visit their Web site at *www.investors.com*.

The *New York Times* (*www.nytimes.com*) provides a business section that includes quotes and charts, a portfolio management tool, and breaking business news.

USA Today (*www.usatoday.com*) features a money section that includes investment articles and news, economic information, and information on industry groups.

The *Wall Street Journal* is the Big Kahuna among investment newspapers, although its authority isn't as unquestioned as it used to be. For subscription information, call 800-778-0840 or visit their Web site at *www.wsj.com*.

Portfolio Management Tools

There are several portfolio management tools that you can use to manage your portfolio. Check out the following Web sites:

Morningstar (*www.morningstar.com*) provides a portfolio setup menu that is easy to use.

Quicken (*www.quicken.com*) offers a variety of financial tools including an excellent portfolio-management program.

Microsoft (*www.money.msn.com*) offers a wealth of financial data.

Quotes (Stocks and Mutual Funds)

American Stock Exchange (*www.amex.com*) offers quoting services on their Web site for stocks that are traded on its exchange.

Microsoft Investor (*www.investor.msn.com*) offers a free stock ticker that you can personalize along with portfolio-tracking tools.

The National Association of Securities Dealers (*www.nasdaq.com*) offers quoting services on their Web site for stocks that are traded on its exchange.

The New York Stock Exchange (*www.nyse.com*) offers quoting services on their Web site for stocks that are traded on its exchange.

PC Quote (*www.pcquote.com*) offers current stock prices, portfolio tracker, company profiles, and broker recommendations.

Business Week (*www.businessweek.com/investor*) features applicable information for researching investment opportunities.

Retirement Planning

60 Plus Association at *www.60plus.org*

American Association of Retired People at *www.aarp.org*

Fifty Plus Net at *www.fifty-plus.net*

Grand Times at *www.grandtimes.com*

Hoover's Online (*www.stockscreener.com*) provides a special module for retirement planning.

InfoSeniors at *www.infoseniors.com*

Money Central (*www.moneycentral.com*) walks you through the process of setting up a retirement plan, including calculating your living expenses and determining your income requirements.

New LifeStyles at *www.newlifestyles.com*

Retirement Net at *www.retirenet.com*

Schwab Investor Profile (*www.schwab.com*) offers an investor's profile questionnaire that matches you to one of six retirement-oriented portfolios.

Senior Living at *www.seniorliving.com*

Senior.com at *www.senior.com*

Senior School at *www.seniorsummerschool.com*

Senior Sites at *www.seniorsites.com*

Tax Assistance

U.S. Tax Code On-Line (*www.fourmilab.ch/ustax/ustax.html*) enables you to access the complete text of the U.S. Internal Revenue Code.

Quicken (*www.quicken.com*) has an extensive investment section that covers stocks, mutual funds, and bonds.

IRS home page (*www.irs.ustreas.gov*) provides official printable tax forms.

Index